# THE COLONIAL ORIGINS OF AMERICAN THOUGHT

## MAX SAVELLE

*Professor of History*
*The University of Washington*

---

### AN ANVIL ORIGINAL

*under the general editorship of*

### LOUIS L. SNYDER

---

D. VAN NOSTRAND COMPANY, INC.

PRINCETON, NEW JERSEY

TORONTO                    LONDON

NEW YORK

FOR
MICHÈLE AND JONNY

_B_
_865_
_S3_

D. VAN NOSTRAND COMPANY, INC.
120 Alexander St., Princeton, New Jersey (*Principal office*); 24 West 40 St., New York. N.Y.
D. VAN NOSTRAND COMPANY (Canada), LTD.
25 Hollinger Rd., Toronto 16, Canada
D. VAN NOSTRAND COMPANY, LTD.
358, Kensington High Street, London, W.14, England

# PREFACE

Where do ideas come from? How did the American way of thinking get started?

Generally speaking, thinking is a response to a particular situation, a quest for answers to problems presented by the struggle to exist and to find the good life in a given environment. To any new situation, or new environment, or new set of experiences, however, men always bring the ideas and habits learned in the *milieu* from which they come. Thus, in a new land, they naturally seek first to apply the intellectual tools—the ideas—that they have brought with them. If these ideas do not work in the new situation, the newcomers must invent new ideas to fill the new needs or modify the old ones in such ways as to make them effective in the new environment. From the adaptation of old ideas and institutions and the invention of new ones, there emerges a set of ideas and attitudes that—while having some of the features of the intellectual heritage—is, like a new human being, essentially and effectively new.

So it was in colonial Angloamerica. The first settlers, who came from England, started in to build their new societies with the political, social, religious, and economic ideas that they brought with them from the mother country. But the new land required new ways; the new challenges required new responses. The result was the invention of new ways of thinking and a great deal of adaptation of the old ways. Then, with the arrival of hundreds of thousands of non-English Europeans with non-English ideas, the intellectual heritage became a mixed one, in its turn to be adapted to the New World experience and fused with the newly emerging "mind" of Angloamerica. It was out of this synthesis of heritages, adaptations, and inventions that the

3

characteristically American ways of thinking were born.

The origins of American thought, therefore, are to be found in the thinking of the first settlers and their sons and grandsons as they found themselves compelled to modify old ideas and create new ones to meet the challenges of the search for the good life in the North American wilderness. There are many English and European strains in American thought. But the mind of this society is, essentially, neither European nor English: it is American; it had its origin and its first growth in the colonial phase of the American experience.

MAX SAVELLE

*Seattle, Washington*

# TABLE OF CONTENTS

# Part I

# THE COLONIAL ORIGINS
# OF AMERICAN THOUGHT

# — 1 —

# THE ORIGINS OF AMERICAN POLITICAL THOUGHT

The roots of American political ideas reach back to old England, the England of the feudal era, to a time centuries before America was discovered. For it was in the feudal era, in the course of the struggle of the feudal nobles to preserve their ancient privileges against the encroachments of the laws and the authorities of the emerging integral political state, symbolized by the king, that English —and American—ideas of the rights of the citizen against the state were first conceived.

**The Theory of Imperial Relationships.** The Englishmen who first settled in America thought of their new societies as mere extensions of the society of old England, and of themselves as Englishmen with all the rights of Englishmen, exactly the same as those of their fellow-countrymen who remained in England. In other words, English society was one, whether on one side of the ocean or the other. This assumption was shared by Englishmen, too, and by the English government; it was made explicit in that famous phrase in Queen Elizabeth I's charter to Walter Raleigh for the Settlement of Virginia, that they "should have all the privileges of free denizens and persons native of England, in such manner as if they were born and personally resident in our said realm of England."

This basic idea persisted, in the minds both of Englishmen in England and of Englishmen in America, right down to the time of the American Revolution. Furthermore, this sense of oneness with Englishmen everywhere was the psychological basis for a deep and unifying loyalty to "the British nation." Even as late as 1756 Benjamin Franklin wrote to Governor William Shirley of Massachusetts (*see Reading No. 1*) that "I look upon the colonies as so many counties gained to Great Britain" and that "the British Subjects on this side of the water (should be) put . . . on the same footing with those in Great Britain. . . ."

At the beginning it was assumed that English laws, particularly the Common Law, applied in the colonies, and there always existed the right of appeal from the courts of a colony to the supreme court of the Empire, the so-called "law lords" of the Privy Council in England, presided over by the Lord High Chancellor. It presently appeared, however, that it would be impossible to apply all the laws passed by Parliament to the colonies, especially laws obviously dealing with local situations in England itself, so the legal officers of the Crown eventually ruled that no law passed by Parliament applied to the colonies unless they were specifically included under its terms in the text of the law itself.

Of particular interest to the mother country was the fact, discovered in the second half of the seventeenth century, that these new colonial economic units could be of enormous profit to England. In order to channel these profits into the coffers of the mother country and its citizens, therefore, Parliament—following the ideas of the general ideology known as mercantilism—passed a series of so-called "Navigation Laws" and "Acts of Trade" regulating the commerce and the internal economies of the colonies. Moreover, the Crown set up a congeries of institutions in England for the control of the colonial governments and for the administration of the Empire, the most notable of which was the so-called Board of Trade. In doing so, England in effect created a code of laws and institutions applicable to American Englishmen to which the citizens of England were not subject. In other words, while the theory was that the empire was one society on the two sides of the water, the practice was one that assumed a gross difference between the colonial societies and that of the mother country.

As time went on, the colonists experienced a resentment against all the features of this system except those that provided bonuses and other encouragements to certain aspects of the colonial economies and military and naval protection against foreign and Indian enemies. Thus, if the mother country thought of the colonies as mere appendages to English society for which special laws must be made, special institutions created, and special political policies and instruction devised, the Americans themselves were steadily coming more and more to look upon their societies and their governments as different from those of England and to formulate their own rationalizations of their institutions and their political objectives. They thought of themselves as Englishmen, with all the rights of Englishmen, to be sure, but they were Englishmen in a new set of circumstances, circumstances that compelled them, as they thought, to construct new institutional frameworks and formulate new interpretations of old English political ideas to fit new conditions and new experiences. Only they, they thought, so far away from the mother country in space, time, and experience, could understand their problems; only they could formulate the solutions to those problems. This view implied a measure of colonial autonomy—so great a measure, indeed, as to mean, to many of their more conservative compatriots, both in England and America, practical independence.

It was as a matter of expediency, chiefly, that while the consciousness of difference was growing, the colonies adopted the practice of appointing agents to reside in London and to represent the interests of the colonies in their relationships with the central government, whether in Parliament, with the Board of Trade, or, more informally, with merchants and other interested parties in England. The functions of these agents were those of a sort of consular or diplomatic agent, involving a combination of negotiation, lobbying, and personal influence. The most famous of these agents were Jeremiah Dummer, who represented several colonies in London early in the eighteenth century, and Benjamin Franklin, who represented several in the third quarter of the century.

Dummer wrote a famous booklet, called *A Defence of the New England Charters* (*see Reading No. 7*), in which he gave expression to a theory of the relationships that he thought ought to exist between colonies and mother

country. Trying to forestall a movement to revoke or
modify the old charters of the quasi-autonomous New
England colonies, Dummer argued that the colonies were,
and would be, most profitable to the mother country if
left free to regulate their own commerce as only they could,
since, he said,

> The Trade of a young Plantation is like a tender Plant, &
> should be cherish'd with the fondest Care; . . . The proper
> Nursery for this Plant is a free Government, where the Laws
> are Sacred, Property secure, & Justice not only impartially
> but expeditiously distributed. . . .

As an expression of colonial theory as to the nature of
and the interrelationships of the Empire, this little book
may be called one of the earliest statements of an American theory of colonial autonomy within the Empire that
was to flower later in the thought of the political philosophers of the decade just preceding the American Revolution.

The problem that had gradually emerged in this area
of American political thinking was that of the true constitutional nature of the relationships between the colonies and
the central government or the Empire as a whole. Where
did the rightful, constitutional authority of the colonial
government begin, and where did that of the Imperial
government end? Or how far did the authority of the
Imperial government extend into the internal affairs of the
colonies? In this problem in theory and practice are
found the origins of the later problem of the true constitutional relationships that exist between the states of the
American union (the theory of states' rights) and the union
as a whole (the theory of "federalism" exemplified, say,
by John Marshall).

**The Political Ideology of the Colonial Whigs.**   At the
moment of their first founding, the colonial societies had
no local or provincial governments of their own. They
had to invent their own forms and construct their own
institutions, as best they might, out of the fragments of
ideas and institutions they brought with them, in such a
way as to meet the challenge of the new conditions in
which they found themselves. The internal political history
of the English colonies from founding to independence is

thus a history of the erection of new governments, in a new land, conformably with a new set of conditions.

As a broad generalization it may be stated that the way of thinking on political matters that emerged out of this experience was essentially a "Whig" ideology. That is to say that, in general, the evolution of American political institutions centered, during the colonial period, about the steady increase in the power of the representative, or popular, or "commons" arm of government—a concentration of power that reached its culmination in the state constitutions of the Revolutionary era. The ideology that justified the preponderance, if not the supremacy, of the representative "commons" section of government, as against the Crown or the aristocratic section (in England, the Lords) may properly be called a "Whig" ideology.*

By the beginning of the eighteenth century, for example, the colonial assemblies were consistently maintaining that they were endowed with all the rights and immunities of the House of Commons in England. These included the right to elect their own speakers, freedom of speech in their debates, the right to sit upon the qualifications of their members, and personal immunity from arrest while in session. John Randolph, speaker of the Virginia House of Burgesses, gave this set of ideas eloquent expression in 1736, when he said that

> Freedom of Speech is the very Essence of their Being, because, without it, nothing could be thoroly debated, nor could they be looked upon as a Council; an Exemption from arrests, confirm'd by a Positive Law, otherwise their Counsels and Debates might be frequently interrupted, and their Body diminished by the Loss of its Members; a Protection for their Estates, to prevent all Occasions to withdraw them from the necessary Duty of their Attendance; a Power over their own Members, that they may be answerable to no other Jurisdiction for anything done in the House; and a sole Right of determining all Questions concerning their own Elections, lest

---

* The American "Whigs," as described here, must not be thought of as having been identical with the English Whigs of the same period. They differed in a number of ways. What they had in common—and this was basic—was their belief, on both sides of the ocean, in the supremacy of the "commons" section of government.

contrary Judgments, in the Courts of Law, might thwart or destroy Theirs.

Central to the ideology of the American Whigs was the concept of individual "liberty"—the liberty of the English subject, of which the great defensive institution was representative government, the liberty that must be defended against tyrannical government at all costs. "The Preservation of Liberty," said one writer, "is a Point equally nice with the Preservation of a Ladies Chastity; the first Assaults are to be repell'd with the utmost Fortitude. A Maidenhead, a Fort, or a Constitution, that begins to capitulate, will soon surrender. If the Outworks are once given up, The Citadel cannot be long maintain'd."

In the course of the dialogue between the assemblies and the governors there also appeared the idea of "balanced" government. The Tories had their own ideas of balanced government, but for the Whig theorists it meant a device for checking the power of the governor, or as they put it, a balance between the legislative branch of the government and the executive. The weight of the judiciary in the balance, as yet, hardly entered into the discussion, since it was part of each assembly's program to limit the governor's power of appointment and assume to itself the power to create the courts, which would have meant a considerable degree of control of the courts by the legislature itself. The "balance," to the Whig theorists, should be one between the legislature and the executive.

Among the colonial Whigs were to be found such men as William Smith and William Livingston of New York, John Randolph of Virginia, and David Lloyd of Pennsylvania. The classic American statement of the right of revolution was that pronounced by Jonathan Mayhew in his famous sermon of 1750. But the idea was not new in the colonies; indeed, it was widely accepted, and had been often expounded, by preachers and others, long before Mayhew—as, for example, in the sermon preached by John Barnard before the Massachusetts governor and legislature in 1746 (*see Reading No. 2*). Barnard cited, as his English precedent, the recourse to arms against James II in 1688.

**The Political Ideology of the Colonial Tories.** The steady movement of political history in colonial America was toward the institutional and ideological realization of the Whig system of thought. But that progress was made against the steady opposition of the American Tories.* This faction, generally of aristocratic complexion, was made up in each colony of those officials and great property-owners who were grouped about the office and the person of the colonial governor. Generally speaking, its members were men of large estates and conservative mind who paid great deference to the majesty and the power of the Crown and who wished, above all things, to preserve the Crown's prerogative, as exercised by the colonial governors, against the steady expansion of the "popular" or "democratical" division of government embodied in the colonial assemblies.

For the Tories, the essential element in the government of the colonies was the prerogative of the Crown. This royal prerogative was a quality that was inherent in the kingship; it was not the gift of the people, and therefore the people could neither diminish it nor take it away. As the Tories interpreted the history of the colonies, all of the colonies had been created by the will and action of the British Crown. The Crown had given them their charters; the Crown had created their governments; what the Crown had created, it might modify or liquidate at will. According to William Keith, one-time governor of Pennsylvania, the colonies were "little dependent provincial Governments," or "so many Incorporations at a distance," completely subservient to the "legal Prerogative of the Crown." Archibald Kennedy considered the colonies parts of the king's royal demesne; they were not subject to Parliament, to be sure, but were entirely subject to the personal, feudal power of the monarch. These men saw in the extension of the power of the colonial assemblies unconstitutional infringements upon the Crown's prerogative and feared, not without reason, that the growth of the assemblies' power, if not checked, must eventually lead to

---

* The American "Tories," like the American Whigs, were not the exact duplicates of their English counterparts. They did hold, as the English Tories did, to the preservation of the power of the Crown against the steady encroachments of the "commons," as manifested in the colonial legislatures.

American independence. Actually, in their defense of the
Crown's prerogative, the American Tories, backed by the
governors' instructions and other pronouncements from
England, claimed much more power for the prerogative
in the colonies than it then enjoyed in England itself.
(*See Reading No. 3.*)

The Tories stood against the popularization of government. They stood for a maintenance, even a strengthening,
of the political connection with the mother country. Above
all, they stood for a maintenance, even a strengthening, of
the royal prerogative. Similarly, they opposed the fight of
the Assemblies for an "independent" judiciary (which
would really be responsible to the Assemblies), and although the judges in England held their appointments
"during good behaviour" and could not be removed, the
American Tories stoutly supported the refusal of the Crown
and the colonial governors to accept such a principle in
the colonies. On the question of taxation, they fought a
losing battle for the idea that the Crown could command
the assemblies to appropriate money or that money, once
appropriated, might be spent by the executive arm without an accounting to the representative house of the legislature. Here is to be seen the origins of a sort of dialectic,
between executive and legislative, that has persisted in
American political history and in American political ideas.

Out of the conflicts of these rival sets of ideas as to the
nature of the colonial and imperial constitutions there
were born many of the ideas that influenced the subsequent
development of American political thought as well as that
of American political history. The American Revolution
was in a real sense a conflict between the two schools of
developing ideas that had had their origin during the colonial period. Even then, although the Whig ideas triumphed
in the winning of American independence, certain ideas
derived from those of the colonial Tories survived and
persisted for at least two centuries.

# — 2 —

# THE ORIGINS OF AMERICAN ECONOMIC THOUGHT

By far the greatest proportion of immigrants to Anglo-america in the colonial period, whether the original English settlers or the later non-English immigrants—Germans, Scots-Irish, and others—were attracted to America by the prospect of getting and owning land. A large minority came for the purpose of engaging in the fishing industry; others, especially those from English and continental European towns, came primarily with the idea of engaging in commercial pursuits. Many of those who entered the colonies as indentured servants came, of course, merely as laboring men with a vague hope of advancement, while the thousands of condemned criminals deported by England to the colonies and the hundreds of thousands of Negro slaves imported from Africa doubtless felt no active motivation whatever, economic or otherwise. Yet among those who deliberately determined to emigrate to America, the motivation that led them to make the great decision was predominantly economic.

While some of the emigrants came from areas still under the influence of the communal economic modes of feudal Europe, most of these earliest Americans were imbued with the spirit of economic individualism that stemmed from the Commercial Revolution. This meant that they accepted the principles of private ownership of property, of individual private profit in economic activity, and of the corporate organization of business enterprise—and also the speculative spirit of early modern capitalism. Central

19

to this way of economic thinking was the assumption of the validity of individual motives, individual activity (which might lead to voluntary corporate organization), and individual profits.

On a national scale, the emerging integral states of western Europe applied this concept of "enlightened self-interest" in their public policies, both with regard to their internal economic life and in the conduct of their international relations. The corpus of ideas that extended the concept of enlightened self-interest to the state as a whole has been called "mercantilism." According to its tenets the state was a sort of great mercantile corporation, whose chief objective it was to sell, or export, more than it bought, or imported. The profits from this favorable balance of trade would then accrue to the people, all of whom would share in the benefits, and the nation would become rich and strong.

It was this generally nationalistic and self-centered way of thinking that led to the enactment, by the English Parliament, of the so-called "navigation laws" regulating American colonial commerce for the net benefit of English merchants. Similarly, the so-called "Acts of Trade" were enacted by Parliament to prevent American manufacturers from competing with manufacturers in England. As the colonies developed, they adopted this inherited way of corporative economic thinking, and enacted many mercantilistic regulations for the governance of their own economic life. But the mercantilist mood was never as strong in the colonies as in England: their "enlightened self-interest" led them in another direction, as we shall see. Furthermore, the mother country's mercantilistic regulation and limitation of colonial manufactures and commerce was a constant and steadily increasing source of resentment in the colonies against the mother country's economic domination. The colonial experience of the Americans was leading them to think along new and more original lines.

**The Folklore of Economic Individualism.**    The ideals of economic individualism received a strong impetus from the experience of the colonists in America. Puritan economic thought, for example, at the beginning was still strongly tinged with the old, scholastic communal ideal, as evidenced by the numerous early laws regulating quality

and prices of commodities, wages, and the antisocial practices of profiteers. But the Puritan economic ideal encouraged thrift and hard work: a righteous man was expected to be a sober and industrious man. Furthermore,
while antisocial business practices were always frowned
upon, if a righteous man accumulated a fortune, it was
taken as a probable sign that God approved of him and
his industry. Again, the Puritans, with their belief in the
economic and social gradations of society, accepted the
idea of "calling," that is, that the trade or occupation a
man was born into—or stumbled into—was the trade to
which God had "called" him for the service of society.
But long before 1700 the plenitude of opportunity and
the visible fact that thousands of men and boys rose from
humble trades and economic circumstances to affluence
had made the idea of "calling" hardly more than a consola-
tion for the poor.

Similarly, in Virginia, whereas the first settlers of the
colony were hardly more than employees of the Virginia
Company, economically supported as well as governed
by the Company in England, the prosperity of the colony
became a reality after the discovery of the possibility of
tobacco cultivation, when land was issued to the settlers in
individual title and they were encouraged to raise their
tobacco individually. The men who became well-to-do, in
all of the colonies, were individuals who had the industry,
the acumen, and the thrifty habit presently to be glorified
by "Poor Richard" in his almanac. The "self-made man"
was a reality of everyday experience; the idea of the self-
made man was only the doctrine of economic individualism
expressed in terms of its expected results.

The most nearly universal vehicle for the articulation of
the folklore of economic individualism was the eighteenth-
century almanac. Of the dozens of these that flourished in
Angloamerica in the eighteenth century, by far the most
eloquent purveyor of this popular mood was *Poor Richard's
Almanack* (*see Reading No. 4*), published by Benjamin
Franklin (and, later, as *Poor Richard Improved,* by Franklin in partnership with David Hall). It was "Poor Richard,"
and others like him, who wrote into American economic
folklore such pithy adages as "Early to bed, and early to
rise, makes a man healthy, wealthy, and wise," "Beware

of little Expence; a small Leak will sink a great Ship," "A Plowman on his Legs is higher than a Gentleman on his Knees," "Penny wise, pound foolish," and "Lost Time is never found again."

**The Natural-Rights Theory of Private Property.**    The folklore of the self-made man was characteristic of the Angloamerican societies of the eighteenth century. Although it is true that in the older settled communities, whether the plantation areas of the south or the commercial cities of the north, economic lines and social strata tended to become fixed, the frontier was always open. New people were constantly coming in to fill up the vacant lands and to introduce new initiative and inventiveness into the economy, and literally hundreds of thousands of them "made good."

But the rationalization of economic individualism was much more than folklore. Its basic ideology was explicitly stated by many an American economic thinker, and by none more clearly, perhaps, than "Philalethes" (probably Elisha Williams) in Massachusetts, whose plea for religious toleration was also an exposition of the natural-rights interpretation of property. (*See Reading No. 5.*)

Such was the logical basis of the strong American conviction that property is a natural right. If the possession of one's property is of the same nature as the possession of one's natural body, obviously, a man's property may not be taken away from him: the right to life and the right to property are identical and, therefore, inseparable.

**Taxation.**    It was this sort of economic thinking that made taxation a matter of such profound and vital interest to practically all Americans. For if a man's property were a part of him, his by natural right, to be disposed of only by his consent and never at the behest of arbitrary government, then taxation, which was a voluntary contribution of the property owner for the support of government, could only be collected with his consent, and not otherwise. Since he could not travel to the seat of government to give his consent in person, his consent must be expressed by his representative, for whom he did, indeed, vote personally.

Taxes were of various sorts in the different colonies. They included taxes upon land, profits, and incomes, excise taxes and poll taxes, and duties upon imports and exports.

Any one of them, in the minds of the colonial thinkers, was thought of as being a surrender of a part of a man's property to the state. The idea that a man has a natural and unalienable right to his property and that his payment to the state must be voluntary (i.e., by consent expressed by his representatives in the legislature) was universally accepted. The most troublesome problem for the theorists was the question where the burden should fall most heavily —upon the landowners or the merchants, upon "estates" in proportion to each man's wealth, or upon all men equally.

There were many other ideas expressed, by many men, on what might be the best form of taxation. Much of the theorizing forecast the debate over taxation of the colonies by Parliament that was to take place after 1763; a few suggestions were advanced, indeed, that Parliament might tax the colonies; but almost all the colonial thinkers on the subject agreed that taxes could be levied only by the representatives of the property owners sitting in the lower houses of the colonial legislatures. Many of the ideas born of these debates became ideas over which men fought when the Revolution came.

**Labor and Wages.**    A vast majority of the men and women who constituted the nuclei of the colonial societies were working people—that is, laborers. There were some middle-class individuals with mercantile interests among the first colonists, and the officials sent to the colonies by England were often "gentlemen" or members of the lesser nobility; but the number of English aristocrats who came to America to establish homes was negligible. It was workers of England, Germany, Northern Ireland, and elsewhere who constituted the vast majority of those who came to America to get a new start in life. It was they, indeed, who built America. With no capital but the labor of their own backs and the land that they were able to acquire, first by the "head-right" system and then by the expansion of their holdings by purchase or marriage, many an immigrant was able to accumulate a competence or even wealth. They knew the value of labor, and they respected it.

As the economy expanded and wages continued to rise despite the inflow of immigrants, the economic theorists became resigned to the necessity of paying high wages for the sake of attracting workers, increasing consuming power, and manning the expansion of commerce. In a surprisingly enlightened essay by "Philopatris," for example, published in the *Maryland Gazette* toward the end of the Seven Years War, this general economic reasoning was very clearly stated. Actually, what Philopatris was trying to do was to show that, after all, there was no conflict between the agrarian interests and the mercantile interests and that they were really interdependent. Incidentally, however, in showing how beneficial to the farmers a prosperous foreign commerce might be, he also presented a fine argument for paying attractive wages to the workers. Increased wages attract more laborers for the conduct of trade, he said, and they also increase purchasing power; increased purchasing power results in higher prices for farm products; increased demand and higher prices raise the value of the farmer's land; from these facts spring a whole host of benefits to the farmers from the prosperity of trade, not to mention the laboring men themselves, who enjoy a higher standard of living!

**Thought about Money and Value.** For the first century or more of their economic history, the colonies had little or no hard money. Such coin as there was came into the colonies from the French, Spanish, and Dutch colonies in the Caribbean area, but even this coin constantly tended to disappear from circulation, either into the secret hiding places of hoarders, or by export to England to help offset the unfavorable balance of trade with the mother country. Exchanges of values in internal trade and external commerce were executed by the actual exchange of goods—that is, by barter. "Barter exchange," however, was practiced only as a matter of sheer necessity: in reality, everyone would have used money if he had had it; and the belief that gold and silver species constituted the only real money was practically universal. It was because of the lack of gold and silver that the colonists turned to the use of paper money as a circulating medium.

There can be no doubt that, despite its fluctuations in value, this paper money was a highly beneficial mechanism for the conduct of business or that it contributed mightily to the rapid expansion of the colonial economy. Yet its successful inauguration and its eventual acceptance by the conservative leaders of colonial economic life called out a vast amount of thinking, both in favor of paper money and against it.

On the side of the creation of a paper currency there stood such thinkers as John Wise, Hugh Vance, Benjamin Franklin, Hugh Borden, and others. Vance, probably the ablest of early American thinkers on the subject, started from the problem inherent in the colonies' unfavorable balance of trade with the mother country—their "shameful balance of debt" with England—and argued powerfully that paper money provided the absolutely necessary medium of exchange.

On the opposite side, opposed to paper money, were such conservative business and professional men as William Douglass, James Logan, Thomas Hutchinson, Cadwallader Colden, and others.

William Douglass, whose argument was fairly typical, insisted that money, to have any worth at all, must have real value; the most ideal commodity for this purpose was silver. He conceded that paper, if it represented a real equivalent value in actual silver bullion, did have its uses. But he saw clearly the dangers of inflation; he had personally suffered losses by the inflation that had characterized the monetary situation in Massachusetts.

Meanwhile, the debate over paper money raised the question of the nature of value, and a number of colonial thinkers turned their attention to this problem. One of the most notable of these was Benjamin Franklin, who, borrowing most of his ideas from the English economist, Sir William Petty, based his advocacy of paper money in Pennsylvania in 1729 upon a "quantity theory" of money and a "labor theory" of value. For the value of any commodity, says Franklin (*see Reading No. 6*), is really determined by the amount of labor that is required to produce it. This is true, he says, even of silver.

**Freedom of International Trade.** Individual economic freedom is akin to collective (national) economic freedom; in retrospect, it appears to have been almost inevitable that the one should have led to the other in colonial America. This did not take place as quickly or as easily as might be supposed, however.

For the first century or more of their history, the co-

lonial societies assumed that government must interfere in
the economy, more or less along the lines envisioned by
the mercantilist way of thinking. Their legal codes are
therefore studded with laws regulating manufactures, commerce, trade practices, wages and labor, and so on. While
there was resentment against the mercantilistic operations
of the British colonial system right from the beginning,
thoughtful men justified and accepted that system on the
ground that it promoted the economic welfare of the entire
empire and that every individual Britisher, Englishman and
colonial alike, benefited from its operations.

As the colonial societies grew, however, they increasingly
came to realize that their long-term economic interests did
not coincide precisely with those of England. The colonists
complained with increasing bitterness against the commercial regulations embodied in the British laws of navigation and trade on the ground that they, as Englishmen,
were thereby subjected to restrictions upon their economic
life that did not apply to Englishmen in England. They
realized, of course, that they could often make better
profits on their tobacco, sugar, rice, and other regulated
commodities by sending them to non-English markets than
they could in the protected markets of England. This implied that they needed a greater freedom of trade than
England was permitting them, and there appeared an
American economic theory that envisioned a degree of
colonial economic specialization and freedom of commerce
never envisioned by British colonial policy. Such a set of
ideas was expressed by one of the American colonial agents
in London, Jeremiah Dummer, for example, in his *Defense of the New England Charters* (*see Reading No. 7*),
written in 1721, at a moment when the British government appeared to be moving in the direction of canceling
the colonial charters and bringing the colonies more directly under the control of the British Crown. Dummer
argued that the colonists had the same right to trade with
non-English markets that Englishmen had in England itself.
As a matter of practical reality, he said, the colonies were
highly valuable to the mother country, chiefly because the
profits from their exports to non-English markets made it
possible for them to buy great quantities of manufactured
goods produced in England—which was probably true.

Cadwallader Colden, governor of the commercially oriented province of New York, realized fully the importance of encouraging the opening of new markets for the New York importers and exporters. (*See Reading No. 8.*) Another American whose economic thinking was running in the direction of a greater degree of colonial economic autonomy, especially a greater freedom of commerce, was Benjamin Franklin. Franklin argued that freedom of commerce for the colonies would not make them rivals of the mother country. On the contrary,

> But in proportion to the increase of the Colonies, a vast Demand is growing for British Manufactures, a glorious Market wholly in the Power of Britain, in which Foreigners cannot interfere, which will increase in a short Time even beyond her Power of supplying, tho' her whole Trade should be to her Colonies; Therefore Britain should not too much restrain Manufactures in her Colonies. A wise and good Mother will not do it. To distress, is to weaken, and weakening the Children weakens the whole Family.

Out of the experiences and the debates of Americans over economic problems in the Colonial period, then, were born many of the economic ideals that have persevered through much of subsequent American history. Such ideas as those of economic individualism, "the self-made man," "no taxation without representation," the advocacy of a flexible currency, freedom of commerce, and many others became firmly rooted, in the course of those debates, in the American "mind." They have remained precious elements in American thinking ever since.

## — 3 —

# THE ORIGINS OF AMERICAN
# SOCIAL THOUGHT

The moods and mores that were the concomitants of the English system of society came to America with the first settlers. In every colony the social institutions and conventions were calculated to reproduce, more or less exactly, those the immigrants had known in the old country. These new societal phenomena were not, however, precise reproductions of English forms. Few of the English aristocracy, for example, ever came to America to settle. The leaders of the first New England settlements were men of the English mercantile and bureaucratic classes; a few of those who went to the Chesapeake area were men of the lesser English gentry. The great preponderance of the immigrants to Angloamerica, throughout the colonial period, were laborers.

Right from the first, the settlers accepted the current English and European differentiation between the "gentry" and the "common sort." As they arrived and established their homes, they tended to move, almost automatically, into social stations corresponding to those they had occupied in England. But as many of them acquired land and other property of their own, and as private wealth accumulated, whether among the merchants of the colonial cities or among the plantation owners of the southern colonies, the members of these wealthy classes assumed all the attributes of a native American aristocracy. Naturally enough, as they became aristocrats the ideology of the stratified society was reinforced in their thinking.

Below the aristocrats in the social scale stood the prosperous farmers (notably in the middle colonies), the small shopkeepers in the towns, the artisans and journeymen, the indentured servants, in that order, from the top downward, and, as the "mudsills of society," the Negro slaves in all the colonies.

This acceptance and rationalization of the stratified society persisted into the eighteenth century, and it characterized the attitudes and thought of such conservative aristocrats as Dr. Alexander Hamilton of Annapolis and William Byrd of Virginia.

**The Ideology of Social Fluidity.** However, there were several profound currents of events at work to break down the stratified structure of society; these forces became especially effective in the eighteenth century.

In the first place, the plenitude of land, the rapid expansion of capital wealth, and the ever-present reality of widespread economic opportunity all combined to make it easy for a man of industry, thrift, and intelligence to accumulate a competence, even a fortune. And as his wealth increased, a man's social status tended steadily to rise. He might even hope to enter the highest levels of society. If he did not quite make it, his sons—especially if they went to college, as many of them now did—might be fairly sure of being accepted as members of the "gentry"—that is, as aristocrats. It was an "open society," marked by social fluidity, in which there was constant movement by its individual members across class lines. Almost anybody, if he worked hard enough and was lucky—or if his children were—could move upward through the grades of society, chiefly by the accumulation of wealth.

In the second place, the frontier tended to have a leveling effect on society in general. Some large landowners there were on the frontier, but most of the frontiersmen in the eighteenth century were small farmers, who literally carved their homesteads out of the forest wilderness. They tended to judge each other not so much by the amount of land one owned as by the success with which he turned the wilderness into flowering farmland. In other words, as a general thing, men were judged by their practical ability rather than by their wealth and pre-existent social status, inherited or otherwise. The social mood and ideal of the frontier tended to be democratic; its influence tended to operate against the establishment of aristocracy and toward the softening, if not the obliteration, of class lines.

A third major factor in the corrosion of the class structure of colonial society was the phenomenal influx of immigrants, most of whom, probably, were non-English in origin. Hundreds of thousands of immigrants came to the colonies in the eighteenth century, from Germany, Ulster (northern Ireland), Scotland, Ireland, France, and Switzerland; a few came from other parts of the American hemisphere; a considerable number migrated from the British West Indies to the mainland. (Hundreds of Negroes came to the English colonies from Africa, too, but they were not full-fledged members of society.) The over-all result of these movements of persons was a significant mixing of national and cultural strains in the colonies. It also had a leveling effect that ultimately corroded the prevailing philosophy of the aristocratic society.

These phenomena, all of which tended toward the breakdown of the aristocratic mood and toward the genesis and growth of social egalitarianism and cosmopolitanism, were commented upon by many observers. The most famous and eloquent of these was Hector St. John de Crevecoeur, a Frenchman who lived in New York from 1754 until 1780. A shrewd observer, Crevecoeur published his observations upon the American social process and ideals in his famous *Letters from an American Farmer,* the best known of which is the one entitled "What Is an American?" (*See Reading No. 9.*) In these essays Crevecoeur romanticized the frontier process and the moods of fluidity and social individualism that characterized American society. But the "melting pot" process he described was a fact; so, too, was the belief in social fluidity and the mood of social egalitarianism that derived from it—and that has been an important factor in the American social mind ever since.

**The Status of Women.** Out of this social fluidity, too, were just beginning to emerge certain new American attitudes toward the status of women.

The earliest settlers, whether in New England or in the southern colonies, never questioned the rightness of the ruling legal precedents and practices of seventeenth-century

England. As one contemporary English commentator explained it,

> Man and wife are one person [*under the law*], but understand in what manner. When a small brooke or little river incorporateth with Rhodanus, Humber or the Thames, the poor rivulet looseth its name, it is carried and recarried with the new associate, it beareth no sway, it possesseth nothing during coverture. A woman as soon as she is married, is called covert, in Latin, *nupta,* that is, veiled, as it were, clouded and overshadowed, she hath lost her streame. . . . To a married woman, her new self is her superior, her companion, her master.

However, the processes of social fluidity and change in America were affecting women as well as men. And there was a growing number of thoughtful Americans who were beginning to formulate more liberal ideas with regard to women's status in society. One of the most articulate of these men was Benjamin Franklin, who, on numerous occasions, showed great respect for the abilities of women and advocated improvements both in their education and in their legal position. He also poked ridicule, on occasion, at the rules—made by men—for the regulation of women's behavior. The most famous example of this was his "Speech of Miss Polly Baker," in which he called "unreasonable" the laws governing adultery. After all, said Polly, she had "brought Five fine Children into the World, at the risk of my Life"; the fines she had paid had hampered her ability to rear them as good citizens! "Can it be a Crime," she continued, "to add to the Number of the King's subjects, in a new Country that really wants People?"

This little piece scandalized many of the staid conservatives, of course. But this was only one aspect—actually, a minor one—of the subtly changing moods of American society relative to the social, intellectual, and legal status of women. The laws were gradually being liberalized with regard to such things as property holding by women, and many women were achieving recognition, even distinction, in business, in farming, in education, in medicine—as midwives and nurses—and in literature.

**Slavery and Its Critics.** Negro slavery was a universally accepted institution in the societies of Anglo-

america in the eighteenth century. This institution had had
its beginning in Virginia in 1619, and it had spread to all
the colonies, especially those south of Pennsylvania, although both slavery and the slave trade existed in all of
them. Throughout the seventeenth century the use of Negro
slaves as a part of the labor force, and the idea that the
Negroes, economically and socially, were "hewers of wood
and drawers of water," were taken for granted by all the
white colonists. By the eighteenth century a considerable
number of writers had given expression to this basic assumption, in discussions of the Negroes and of slavery that
constituted a sort of rationalization of the whole system.
Hugh Jones, of Virginia, for example (*see Reading No.
10*), wrote of the slaves that "Their work . . . is not very
laborious; . . . and when they are free, they know not
how to provide so well for themselves generally; neither did
they live so plentifully nor . . . so easily in their own
Country, where they are made slaves to one another, or
taken captive by their Enemies."

About the beginning of the eighteenth century, there
began to appear a few men who, in the light of the new
and spreading doctrine of the natural "liberty" of all men,
were troubled by the white men's custom of keeping black
men in bondage and even selling them as one might sell
cattle or other chattels. One of the earliest of these, and
one of the most simply eloquent, was Judge Samuel Sewall
of Boston, whose little essay, *The Selling of Joseph*, was
probably the first antislavery tract published in Angloamerica. (*See Reading No. 11*.) Sewall, taking as his text
the biblical story of the selling of Joseph by his brethren,
reasoned that all men, white, black, or otherwise, as the
descendents of Adam, were equally entitled to freedom.
"So that," as he says, "Originally, and Naturally, there is no
such Thing as Slavery." He also argued against slavery on
religious, social, and economic grounds.

As the eighteenth century advanced, the sentiment against
slavery mounted and became increasingly articulate, especially among the Quakers. The Mennonites ("German
Quakers"), indeed, had taken a clear stand against the slave
trade when they resolved, in their Germantown "meeting"
of February 18, 1888, "against the traffic of men-body."
After the turn of the century, there arose two outstanding

Quaker crusaders against slavery in the persons of Anthony Benezet and John Woolman. Woolman, the better known of the two, wrote numerous essays on economic and social questions, with regard to which he consistently taught an application of the principles of Christianity. But his most intense interest and his greatest efforts were directed to the problem of slavery.

True to his religious and philosophical position that Christianity provided the only valid rule for the regulation of human relationships, Woolman found slavery repugnant to the essential principles of the Christian doctrine and spent most of his life preaching the emancipation of the Negro slaves. He never achieved any significant success for his cause during his lifetime, but his ideas—both the negative, against slavery, and the positive, for universal human freedom—were to be amalgamated with those of other men in the current of libertarian thought that has flowed constantly through American history from the eighteenth century to the present.

**America a Refuge.**   In the course of the vast migration of Europeans who left their native lands to seek new homes in America, many—but not all—of the emigrants left Europe to escape some unhappy circumstance in the society they left behind them. Sometimes these circumstances were those of economic poverty; sometimes they centered about political insecurity; often they were religious; many, indeed, of the immigrants from England came as condemned convicts who were permitted this means of escaping terms in jail.

Whatever the motives of the immigrants, many Angloamericans had begun, by the middle of the eighteenth century, to think of their colonial societies as places of asylum for the oppressed of Europe.

This mood coincided exactly with the desire of all the colonies to attract immigrants to build up the labor force; the colonies suffered from a perennial shortage of labor. A number of the colonies took steps, even before the end of the seventeenth century, to legalize the status of non-English immigrants, and Parliament, in 1740, passed a law providing for the naturalization of non-English Protestants in all the colonies.

The very growth and survival of the colonial societies

appeared to depend upon a free and unrestricted immigration. (*See Reading No. 12.*) One of the most common and convincing arguments in favor of paper currencies in the colonies, in fact, was that a scarcity of money kept wages down, whereas an adequate circulating medium would attract laborers from abroad and thus increase both the population and the labor force.

**The Origins of American Sociological Thought.** The population of the colonies increased very rapidly in the eighteenth century, both by immigration and by the exceedingly high birth rate, and this fact attracted the serious attention of a few American thinkers, the most outstanding of whom was Benjamin Franklin.

Franklin was deeply impressed by the rapid expansion of population in the colonies. His most famous essay on the subject, "Observations Concerning the Increase of Mankind, Peopling of Countries, Etc." (*see Reading No. 13*), was an attempt to explain this phenomenon in scientific terms. On the basis of his observations Franklin concluded that population increased more rapidly in agricultural areas than in cities, and more rapidly in America than in Europe. The chief reason he gave was that the cost of living was lower in these productive areas, making it possible for people to marry younger. In America, particularly, the plenitude of land made it possible for workers to become economically independent earlier and, therefore, to begin their families earlier. Franklin believed that this vast, growing market for English manufactures would make the colonies the most profitable segment of the British Empire, and he predicted that America would one day have a greater population than Britain. He also anticipated Malthus with his theory that the increase of population in any country is limited only by the food supply.

Franklin stood almost alone in his effort to explain scientifically the growth of American population. There were numerous others who touched upon the subject; the chief concerns of these writers were generally focused, however, upon the economic aspects of population increase.

Evidently, the ideas that characterized the social thought of the Angloamericans in the eighteenth century were ideas that grew largely out of their day-by-day experience: the ideas of social fluidity that corroded the philosophy of the aristocratic stratified society; the almost imperceptible change in thinking about the status of women; the move for the abolition of slavery; the belief in, and the encouragement of, immigration, coupled with the idealization of America as a land of refuge for the oppressed; and the beginnings of systematic, scientific thought about the nature and the growth of populations. All these, and others, were grounded in the actual experience of the Americans. All, too, were to play important roles in the thinking and the history of America for centuries.

# — 4 —

# ORIGINS OF AMERICAN
# SCIENTIFIC THOUGHT

The first generation of settlers in Angloamerica knew little about the so-called "Copernican" science. Their concept of the physical nature of the universe was still, to a dominant degree, that of the Aristotelian science of the medieval scholastics. But the Copernican Revolution began to show its influence in American scientific thought about the middle of the seventeenth century, in the "Harvard Almanacs." The realistic, observational moods and methods of the new science also showed themselves in the work of such men as John Winthrop, Jr., in Connecticut or John Banister in Virginia, and in the discussion of comets by Samuel Danforth and Thomas Brattle in Massachusetts. The new mood expressed itself vigorously, also, in the rebellion of the Harvard students in 1671 against the use of an antiquated scientific textbook. It is especially notable, about the turn of the century, in the writings of Cotton Mather, who became a member of the British Royal Society, and who, although hardly a practicing observational scientist himself, read much and wrote more in the theory of the natural world and of medicine. Mather's most significant contribution to scientific thought was probably *The Christian Philosopher,* which was essentially a synthesis of scientific knowledge with the tenets of the Puritan religion.

The year before Mather died, the Newtonian system of science was firmly established at Harvard with the creation, in 1727, of the Hollis chair in "natural philosophy" and in the work of Isaac Greenwood, its first occupant. Greenwood may be called the first Newtonian in America, because he emphasized the need for purging science of its bookishness and for teaching and studying it by actual observation, laboratory demonstration, and mathematical verification. With the work of Greenwood's successor in the Hollis chair, Professor John Winthrop, which was paralleled by that of a host of others (mostly non-academicians), Newtonian science in Angloamerica came into its own.

**The Achievements of "Natural Philosophy" and "Physick."** The achievements of science in Angloamerica, despite the elementary nature of its method, were significant. Some, indeed, were highly notable, even brilliant.

In the realm of physics and mathematics, Professor John Winthrop repeated much of the work of the European physicists in the laboratory at Harvard. His most interesting contribution to scientific knowledge and thought derived from his observations of the transits of Mercury (1739) and Venus (1761) and his careful study of the New England earthquake of 1755. Distinguished as these observations were, however, his most significant achievement may have been the number of young men he trained at Harvard to become some of the leading American scientists of a later generation. Benjamin Franklin, the great amateur, studied electricity, heat, and optics; his well-known studies of electricity placed him among the foremost scientists of his time.

In the realm of biology, John Bartram of Philadelphia succeeded in collecting and classifying hundreds of American plants. Cadwallader Colden, Alexander Garden, James Logan, and others experimented with plants. John Clayton of Virginia accurately described many of the plants of his colony in his *Flora Virginica*. Mark Catesby, an Englishman who lived a number of years in the southern colonies, published a massive *Natural History of Carolina, Florida, and the Bahamas* in the 1730's and 1740's. This book was profusely illustrated by beautiful steel-engravings of birds, flowers, and animals. Catesby anticipated John James Audubon by a century.

In the realm of medicine, although doctors still generally followed the ancient theory of the balance of the four bodily humors in their explanation of the basic cause of disease, considerable progress was made in the practical aspects of clinical observation and diagnosis, preventive medicine, quarantine, and the treatment of the mentally ill, simply on the basis of direct observation and the trial-and-error method. The practice of inoculation for smallpox was introduced by Cotton Mather and Dr. Zabdiel Boylston of Boston about 1721. This event alone caused a great deal of thought and discussion, scientific and otherwise, but inoculation proved its validity by its success; men brought smallpox under a high degree of control by this trial-and-error practice, although they never really understood why it worked. The first public hospital in the colonies was established in Philadelphia about the middle of the century.

The high point in the history of medicine in the colonies was reached with the establishment of the chair in medicine at the College of Philadelphia, about 1765, of which Dr. John Morgan was the first incumbent. Morgan, as a "Professor of Theory and Practice of Medicine," and thoroughly trained in Europe, insisted upon the separation of pharmacy and surgery from the practice of medicine itself; he was deeply impressed by the future of scientific research in America. (*See Reading No. 14.*)

In the area of scientific method, also, science in colonial America took certain long steps forward. At the beginning, the Scientific Revolution in Europe was a product of a combination of direct observation of natural phenomena, mathematical measurement of them, and daring speculation based upon these two. There was very little of the "controlled experiment" as modern laboratory scientists know it, although the work of Galileo, Harvey, Boyle, and others may be said to have laid the foundations for its later development. There was very little, if any, genuine laboratory experimentation behind the spectacular theories of Sir Isaac Newton, and John Locke's *Essay Concerning the Human Understanding* was apparently written upon the basis of Locke's personal thinking, without the slightest contact with any experiment or experience other than Locke's own reading and day-by-day observation of humanity.

In Angloamerica, too, speculation or "thought" was an integral part of scientific method. Much of the scientific learning achieved there was derived from direct observation of the phenomena of nature. In the course of the eighteenth century, however, more and more scientific work was done in laboratories and by controlled experiments and was based less and less upon the reading of books or even the simple observation of natural phenomena—as witness the work of Professor Winthrop in physics, Benjamin Franklin in his studies of electricity, Dr. John Lining in his studies of metabolism, James Logan in his study of sex in plants, and numerous others. The close and measured observation of natural phenomena was still basic, of course, but the experimental method, by the middle of the eighteenth century, was clearly on its way.

**Early American Scientific Theory.** Much of the scientific "thought" that went on, if such it may be called, was sheer guesswork. Thus, many serious individuals "thought" saltpeter should be a sovereign ingredient of many fancied remedies; the great Cadwallader Colden, who was a genuine scientist, wrote many thoughtful letters and papers upon the efficacy of "Tar Water" as a cure for human ills; such scientific thinkers (not to say genuine scientists) as Thomas Prince fabricated explanations out of the wholly imaginary "caverns" of the earth and God-impelled disturbances in them. Doctor William Douglass, on the other hand, a distinguished doctor, was convinced, as a medical scientist, that inoculation for smallpox was a dangerous error—a scientific opinion that he, himself, later abandoned when convinced by the evidence that the principle of inoculation was scientifically valid.

Professor Winthrop, perhaps more than anyone else in colonial America, exemplifies the scientific mood of the eighteenth century in his studies of natural phenomena, and he was said to be one of the few men in America—possibly the only one—who thoroughly understood Sir Isaac Newton's *Principia Mathematica.* He correctly believed that time on the earth, and the distance of the planets from the earth, could be more accurately measured by studies of eclipses. His study of the New England earthquake of 1755 (*see Reading No. 15*) brought him, contrary to his New England predecessors, to the correct conclusion that earthquakes are caused by undulations in the earth's crust. His careful scientific explanation brought him into conflict with the leaders of religion, as we shall see.

Benjamin Franklin, surely the greatest scientist Colonial

America produced, achieved international fame not only by his experiments, but also by the conclusions and the practical inventions that sprang from them. Thus, he formulated the theory—and proved—that lightning was electricity (*see Reading No. 16*); he named "positive" and "negative" electricity; he studied heat and invented the "Franklin stove"; he studied optics and invented bifocal spectacles. In his scientific thinking, Franklin accepted the Newtonian corpus of science and encouraged many other scientists—doctors, botanists, mathematicians, and many others—to carry forward the frontiers of scientific knowledge and thought. One of his most distinguished disciples, David Rittenhouse, would one day advance an amazing theory of life on other planets—a theory widely accepted among scientists of the twentieth century.

Cadwallader Colden was undoubtedly the most thoroughgoing scientific theorist in the colonies. He was an experimenter and observer in medicine, physics, and botany; but he did his most impressive thinking in the realm of theoretical physics. For he was bold enough to try to explain the nature of the force of gravity, as Newton had not been willing to do, as a sort of "field" surrounding and emanating from each mass of matter. He also attempted to explain life in organic matter in terms of "fermentation"; and he arrived at something approaching a materialistic explanation of the movement of the masses of the universe in his *Principles of Action in Matter*. (*See Chapter 6.*) Colden was a genuine philosopher of science as well as a theoretical physicist. Although it would be difficult to specify his influence upon later American scientists, Colden must be recognized, despite his numerous "near misses" of the true scientific explanation of things, as one of the originators of American scientific thought.

**Thought about Science.** So far, we have been considering the thought-content of science itself, or systems of thought resting upon science. It is necessary, however, to examine briefly the thought that was developing in America about science.

In the first place, it must be noted that, as science came to America, many men looked upon it as a new way of knowing God. Such thinkers, notably Rev. Cotton Mather, welcomed science and its method as leading to a clearer understanding of God's works and his "natural" laws. Himself a scientist of no mean ability, Mather advised the younger members of the ministry that "What we call Natural Philosophy, is what I must encourage you to spend much more Time in the Study of."

On the other hand, a good many realized that many of the findings of science and of its implications ran counter to some of the statements in the Bible or to the assumptions of the orthodox theologies. Thus, the religious rationalists argued that, if the universe operates according to natural laws, which are the laws of God, the miracles related in the Bible simply could not have happened, since they would have had to be violations of natural laws, and God would not violate his own laws. Similarly, if man is a rational creature, as science seemed to show, that fact alone cast doubt upon the Calvinist doctrine that man is vile, helpless to do good or to choose between good and evil without God's aid.

Thought of this sort led logically to the conclusion, not so much that religion itself should be rejected, but that the tenets of religion must be modified in the light of the new truth revealed by scientists. The effects of this influence of science upon religion will be described in Chapter 5.

In similar fashion, but much more positively, the findings and the implications of science had a powerful influence upon Angloamerican thinking about economics, social phenomena, and politics. It might even be said that science was in large measure responsible for the eighteenth-century beginnings of what later came to be called the "social sciences."

The scientists were increasingly convinced that man, as a rational creature, was capable of understanding the facts and the laws of nature. Understanding them, he could control them for the benefit of men, as Franklin did with his lightning rod. This view meant that man and his society could achieve an unlimited progress: faith in progress was one of the hallmarks of the eighteenth-century Enlightenment. All that was necessary was that the scientists be left free to study nature, to speculate, and to invent. Most of all, they themselves must find ways and means to exchange their findings and their thought, so that they might learn from each other.

Science, indeed, colored many different aspects of American intellectual life, including the growing self-consciousness of Americans about the future of their land. Many American scientists—for example, John Bartram and Lewis Evans —concentrated their studies upon the natural phenomena of America; and in 1765, just at the end of the colonial period, Dr. John Morgan of Philadelphia could say that

> This part of the world [*America*] may be looked upon as offering the richest mines of natural knowledge yet unriffled, sufficient to gratify the laudable thirst of glory in young inquirers into nature.

**Popular Science and Pseudo-Science.**    At the opposite end of the intellectual spectrum from the high and esoteric philosophical lucubrations of, say, Cadwallader Colden stood the scientific thought and the pseudo-scientific folk-lore of the uneducated.

The chief vehicles of science among this popular audience were the annual almanacs and the weekly newspapers. In the former there was a quantity of genuine scientific information, for the almanacs contained schedules of the phases of the moon and the rising and falling of the tides, verses upon science, predictions of eclipses, and prescriptions for various types of illness. The last named were probably widest of the mark; they often recommended the use of such "medical" elements as saltpeter, cobwebs, and dung. Despite its "old-wives'" nature, however, much of the information brought to the people through this medium was scientifically sound and practically useful. Furthermore, the almanacs warned the people against gullibility and taught them to test all astonishing and purportedly magic phenomena by the facts. Nathaniel Ames' *Astronomical Diary* for 1747, for example, published "an Essay on Conjuration & Witchcraft" (*see Reading No. 17*), in which the readers were warned, "But we are not to believe such Reports, unless the Evidence of the Truth of the Fact be equal to the Strangeness of the Thing."

Science and scientific rationalism had come to stay. Intellectual advance was measured by the pace of science and of its implications in all the areas of human thought. It would be difficult to exaggerate the importance of science and its implications as constituting one of the major matrixes in which later American thought had its origins.

# — 5 —

# ORIGINS OF AMERICAN
# RELIGIOUS THOUGHT

The original body of religious thought in Angloamerica was that of English Protestantism, which had two major divisions: the Anglican in the southern colonies and the Puritan in New England. Another Protestant form, that of the Dutch Reformed Church, was the accepted religion in the Dutch settlements on the Hudson and Delaware Rivers. English Puritanism and the Dutch Reformed faith were basically Calvinist in their religious doctrines; Anglicanism, while it contained many elements of Calvinist and even Lutheran doctrine, still retained much of the old Roman Catholic theology and practice. These Protestant sects differed from each other surprisingly little in their essential Christian beliefs. Their differences, which were, of course, very important to them, were differences in interpretation of details of faith and practice that seem surprisingly unimportant to the twentieth-century mind. What they had in common, as against the authoritarianism and the priestly organization of the Roman Catholic Church, was their concentrated emphasis upon the nature of salvation as an individual experience involving a supposed direct contact of God with the individual without the necessary intervention of a priest or any other worldly authority whatsoever.

The Anglicans were settled chiefly in the southern colonies and the English islands in the West Indies. They simply carried with them the religion they knew in England. Anglicanism in these colonies was an extension of the Anglicanism of England; the colonists there never thought of themselves either as in religious revolt or as in any way changing the religion in which they had been reared. The Puritans of the northern colonies, on the other hand, thought of themselves, at first, as Anglicans charged with the awful responsibility of completing the reformation of the Anglican Church, and then, later, as destined to perfect the Reformation in America outside the Anglican fold.

All of these Protestant sects considered themselves as essentially conservative, and they were. They sought to conserve the values of an older time: the Anglicans, to preserve their supposedly ancient Anglican views against the "dissenters," on the one side, and the Roman Catholics on the other; the Puritans, to purge Christianity of the accretions and corruptions of the centuries and return to the simple, directly spiritual religion of Christ and his disciples.

**The Process of Religious Change.**　As the population of Angloamerica grew, the number of different Christian sects multiplied. From England itself came Baptists and Quakers; from Scotland and northern Ireland came Presbyterians. The number of Catholics in Maryland steadily increased, and Catholics appeared in several of the cities along the coast. From Brazil came a congregation of Jews in 1653, and their number was steadily increased by later groups from Europe. Most important, toward the end of the seventeenth century there began a stream of immigrants from the continent of Europe, as we have seen, who included a variety of European sects—Lutherans, Moravians, Mennonites, Dunkers, Schwenckfelders, and numerous others, to which should be added a considerable number of French Huguenots.

Many of these sects were "pietists"; the chief emphasis in their religions was upon piety, or the subjective, emotional union of the individual with God. Such were the pietists among the Lutherans ( a minority, of course; most Lutherans followed the formal doctrine and practice of the Lutheran Church and scoffed at the pietists); such, also, were the Mennonites and the Moravians, and others.

Another factor making for change was the frontier. The frontiersman, living with his family in a cabin often many miles from the nearest village, was likely to find it next to impossible to attend the village church or to be in touch with its pastor, even when they happened to be of his denominational persuasion. The frontiersman was not irreligious; the fact of distance and the pressing nature of the chores of his daily existence simply isolated him from the usual community religious practices. The frontiersman's children, reared in such isolation, were likely to be even less concerned with religion than he was. The inevitable result of this combination of circumstances was a certain degree of religious indifference. On the other hand, as population grew and the spaces were filled in, churches appeared—Baptist, Presbyterian, Lutheran—to combat this indifference and to bring religious activity within reach of the frontiersmen.

A third factor making for religious change was the influence of science upon religious thought. The widely diffused concept of a universe that operates according to natural law stood in logical disagreement with the belief in miracles, for example. The eighteenth-century scientists' faith in human reason as one of the natural phenomena characteristic of human beings tended to corrode the Calvinist doctrine of the vileness and the helplessness of man. Reason itself seemed to prompt the belief that a kindly God would not arbitrarily condemn half of his creatures to hell-fire and damnation, thus undermining the Calvinist doctrine of predestination.

**Rationalism in Religion.** The impact of the implications of science upon religion had the effect of placing more and more emphasis upon the place of reason, or intelligence, in religious thought. Many preachers arose to apply the tests of science and "reason" to the old religious beliefs, with the result that there took place among them a steady corrosion of the beliefs in miracles or in witchcraft. Some challenged the doctrine of predestination; some even went so far as to question the doctrine of the Trinity and to preach a doctrine of the ultimate salvation of all men.

Jonathan Mayhew, for example, pastor of the West Church in Boston, whose own native rationalism was bolstered by a thorough reading of the English rationalists along with Rousseau and Voltaire, was thoroughly convinced of the dignity of man and the authority of individual reason:

It is by our reason that we are exalted above the beasts of the field. It is by this, that we are allied to angels, and all the glorious intelligences of the heavenly world: Yea, by this we resemble God himself. It is principally on account of our reason, that we are said to have been created in the image of God.

Mayhew went on to attack the doctrine of predestination, particularly the condemnation of newborn babies, as absurd. He further implied that Jesus of Nazareth was a man, and he openly criticized the doctrine of the Trinity, thus laying the foundation of Unitarianism in America.

Charles Chauncy, another rationalist, also rejected the doctrine of predestination as unreasonable. God is good, wrote Chauncy, and desires the happiness of his creatures; therefore, all men will eventually be saved. This was the basic idea of American Universalism. Chauncy abhorred the emotional excesses of the Great Awakening and taught his people that "There is such a thing as real religion, let the conduct of men be what it will; and 'tis, in its nature, a sober, calm, reasonable thing. . . ." (*See Reading No. 18.*) And Samuel Quincy repeated the same sentiment when he said that "Christianity is then a rational Religion, and those who deny it can, or ought to be maintained upon rational Principles, do in Effect give it up."

There were many other rationalists, often called "Arminians" (after the Dutch religious leader, Jacob Arminius) because they believed in the rational capacity of men freely to choose between good and evil. Actually, the growth of rationalism in religion constituted a sort of religious revolution, since it represented a turnabout from the Calvinist concept of man as vile and helpless to one that found men to be rational, dignified, self-directing creatures, not utterly dependent upon God, but in large measure responsible for their own destiny. It was a new type of individualism in religion. Every individual, according to the rationalists, must think for himself; he must make his own decisions; the ultimate fate of his soul was largely (but not entirely, of course) in his own hands.

**The Great Awakening.** At the opposite end of the spectrum of religious thought from the high intellectualism of the rationalists stood the nonrational emotionalism of the Great Awakening.

The Great Awakening was a wave of revivalism that swept through the colonies during the third, fourth, and fifth decades of the eighteenth century. It was a sort of American counterpart to the rise of Methodism in England and of pietism in Germany. It can hardly be said to have been inspired by these parallel movements, although George Whitefield, one of the English Methodists, made a series of tours through the colonies, beginning in 1739, and gave a great boost, by his eloquence, to the work of American preachers of the revival.

The Great Awakening had begun in the colonies in the 1720's with the preaching of Theodore Frelinghuysen, a preacher of the Dutch Reformed Church in New Jersey, who attacked the stodgy, conventional orthodoxy of his colleagues and stirred the emotions of his hearers toward an acceptance of "conversion." William Tennent, a Presbyterian, preached a similar "religion of the heart" in Pennsylvania: James Davenport and Jonathan Edwards preached a similar appeal in New England, and Samuel Davies carried the revivalist torch in Virginia.

The Great Awakening, then, was one of the most profound religious experiences of the American people in the eighteenth century. Out of it there emerged the evangelical tradition in American religion; out of it, also, there emerged a religious individualism that has persisted and that has carried over into political and economic thought as well.

**The Voices of Religious Orthodoxy.** It is to be remembered, of course, that the great mass of the people in the colonies were hardly touched, either by the rationalism of the Enlightenment, on the one hand, or by the emotionalism of the Great Awakening, on the other. The great bulk of the people, in other words, remained orthodox in their religious beliefs, and their ministers, such, for example, as Rev. Jonathan Dickinson (*see Reading No. 19*), continued to preach the doctrines of the "old-time religion" that had come down to them from preceding centuries. Some of the conservative preachers, however, challenged by the emotionalism of the Great Awakening, set out to defend the orthodox way from the forces of a too great emotionalism, without, however, going over to the opposite extreme of rationalism. These preachers and their followers, generally called the "Old Lights" as against the "New

Lights" of the Great Awakening, opposed the radical emotionalism and popularizing tendencies of revivalism. Thus, Thomas Clap, President of Yale, preached and wrote with power for the preservation of orthodoxy; Commissary Dawson, head of the Anglican Church in Virginia, did what he could to limit the spread of the awakening among the Presbyterians in the western parts of that colony.

Paradoxically, the greatest of all the conservative religious leaders was Jonathan Edwards, whom we have already met as a leader of the Great Awakening. But Edwards, who was pastor of the Congregational Church at Northampton, Massachusetts, and, in the last year of his life, president of Princeton College, was not really at one with the Great Awakeners. The heart of his religion was a strict doctrinal Calvinism, as against a general carelessness of doctrine among the other Awakeners, and since—which is more important still—Edwards was seeking, even in his appeal to the emotions, or "religious affections," to preserve Calvinism by propounding a philosophy that harmonized this doctrine with the natural world revealed by Newton and Locke. In other words, Edwards tried to preserve, or conserve, the old Calvinistic wine of the absolute omnipotence of God and the utter dependence of man in the new bottles of eighteenth-century science and empiricism. (*See Reading No. 20.*)

In practice, religious conservatism manifested itself in many other ways, as when James Parker, a printer of New York, was forced to disavow a deistic article published in his paper or when Rev. Samuel Hemphill of Philadelphia was silenced by the Presbyterian Synod because of his liberal preaching. Religious conservatism meant a devotion to the preservation of religious orthodoxy against the new currents in religion, both of rationalism and of extreme religious emotionalism. Needless to say, this mood has never died out of American thought.

**The Origins of American Religious Toleration.**    One of the most striking and typical characteristics of American religious thought is the broad, almost universal, acceptance of the idea of religious toleration.

This characteristic has not always prevailed. Very few of the first generation of settlers believed in religious toleration; indeed, the official attitude in most of the first colonies was distinctly intolerant of dissent from the established religious outlook, whether it was Puritanism in Massachusetts or Anglicanism in Virginia. The three outstanding exceptions were the colony of Rhode Island, founded under the leadership of Roger Williams and other dissenters; Maryland, founded by the Barons Baltimore, Charles and Cecilius Calvert; and, later, Pennsylvania, founded by the Quakers under the leadership of William Penn.

Roger Williams, the great morning star of religious toleration in America, was a dissenter who had felt the whip of religious persecution, both in England and in America. He came to the conclusion, as he said, that "God doth not require" worship in any particular way or according to any particular, fixed set of ideas. Williams wrote a number of famous tracts and letters defending and expanding this idea, and he wrote into the charter of the colony of Rhode Island both the principle of freedom of conscience and the institutional separation of Church and State. Williams' thought about toleration was of a negative, permissive kind; even so, he was far ahead of his time.

With William Penn and the other Quakers, the doctrine of religious toleration becomes a positive principle of listening to and learning from what other men have to say. By the middle of the eighteenth century this positive sort of religious freedom was widely accepted throughout the colonies—although not yet by all colonists. Jonathan Mayhew, for example, the great rationalist preacher of Boston's West Church, interpreted the right to religious freedom on the basis of natural right:

> So that it is not left to the option of Christians whether they will relinquish their natural liberty in religious matters, or not; they are commanded to assert it. God has given us abilities to *judge even for ourselves what is right:* and requires us to improve them. He forbids us to *call any man master upon earth.* And as he has forbidden us to submit implicitly to the dictates of any man, so he has also explicitly forbid all Christians to assume or usurp any authority over their brethren.

Archibald Kennedy, of New York, in a famous theoretical address to his son, expressed much the same idea:

I allow you Freedom of Conscience, to think, and judge for yourself; and I likewise allow you Freedom, if not entirely from all Manner or [*of?*] Influence, yet from the Dominion of Human Authority, in thinking and judging for yourself.

In the thought of Mayhew and Kennedy is to be seen a sort of synthesis of the religious doctrine of individual inspiration with the influence of science that proclaimed the principle of intellectual freedom—of individual investigation and the communication of scientific findings for the sake of learning and the advancement of scientific progress. It constitutes a sort of high-water mark in the growth of the idea of religious and intellectual freedom that had developed from the practical experience of the Angloamericans, the religious ideas of such men as Williams and Penn, and the rationalistic desirability of intellectual freedom implicit in the work of the scientists. Benjamin Franklin could demonstrate, with entire accuracy, that religious toleration in the colonies was considerably more extensive than it was in England, and William Livingston of New York could describe religious toleration as one of the outstanding characteristics of American society. (*See Reading No. 21.*)

Thus, in the course of the religious experiences of the colonial Americans there were set in motion the four major traditions in the history of American religious thought: the orthodox, the rationalistic, the evangelical, and that of complete individual religious freedom.

# — 6 —

# ORIGINS OF AMERICAN
## PHILOSOPHY

Philosophy is—or should be—the apex of the pyramid of human thought, since its function is to find the ultimate answers to the riddle of existence. The problem it seeks to resolve is that of the true nature of the universe and of man's relationship to it, and, in the light of these, the best way to live in order to find the "good life."

In the first century of the history of Angloamerica, there was little of the sort of systematic thinking upon this most profound and most necessary of all intellectual problems that may properly be called philosophy. The one exception was Puritanism, considered in its philosophical aspects. Indeed, most of the philosophical thinking that went on during the colonial period was done chiefly in the interest of rationalizing (that is, logically explaining and justifying) religious positions already taken.

And yet, as the Angloamerican societies expanded and became more sophisticated, and as the new currents of European thought made themselves felt in Angloamerica, several clear and significant strains of philosophy appeared among American thinkers. It is in the thought of these American intellectuals of the eighteenth century that the origins of American philosophies are to be found.

**Puritanism as a Philosophy.** Puritanism, as a philosophy, was a system of thought that explained the universe in Calvinistic terms. It was, in effect, a sort of derived Platonism. According to its explanation of the nature of things, God, the great creator, had created two sorts of reality, one spiritual and one material. The earth, of course, was material. Man, at the beginning, had had within him both natures: he was material—an animal, a "creature"—but he also had a spiritual soul. Adam, the first man, under the subversive influence of Satan, God's eternal enemy, had rebelled against his creator, and God had punished Adam and his descendants forever by depriving the human soul of its capacity to perceive the spiritual good without God's special help, rendered to each individual personally. Men could thus recover their original spiritual nature, but only by the gracious intervention, in each individual case, of God himself. Thus, the Puritan philosophy presents a dualistic universe of matter and spirit, presided over by its creator, an omnipotent and omniscient God. Man's relationship to the universe was that of a creature utterly dependent upon his creator. The ethical outcome of this explanation of reality was that man finds the good life only in the full, whole-hearted acceptance of his dependence upon God and of God's guidance. But those happy ones who found the truly good life were only God's "elect" —only those whom God, in his grace, had "saved," those whose spiritual souls had been regenerated by the touch of God's hand and whose spiritual eyes had been opened. The others, the "unregenerate," were still creatures of sin, blind to good and incapable of choosing it, whom God, in his inscrutable justice, would punish for their sins by condemning them to the eternal fires of hell.

**The Impact of Science and the Newtonian-Lockean Synthesis.** The inexorable march of time, experience, and ideas was corroding the pristine purity and logical rigidity of the Calvinistic Puritan philosophy. Among common men, the frontier experience had forced upon Americans a sense of the secular and the practical. It had directed men's attentions from books and speculation to things and to the everyday struggle for existence; it had scattered the population beyond the reach of the social control exercised by the closely-packed communities in the towns; and it had diluted the willingness of men and women to testify in open meeting that God had touched their souls. On the other hand, the impact of Sir Isaac Newton's theory of natural law and of John Locke's theory of knowledge was having a revolutionary effect upon the speculative thinking of the intellectuals of the entire western world, including America. Locke, especially, in *An Essay Concerning the Human Understanding,* provided science and scientific thought with a systematic explanation of how men know—an epistemology that brilliantly rationalized and justified the kind of knowledge of the outside world that the scientists themselves were acquiring. Such an epistemology, coupled with the Newtonian cosmology, the philosophers of the eighteenth-century Enlightenment could not ignore. Indeed, they seized upon the Newtonian-Lockean synthesis with avidity, since it so perfectly fitted their own empirical explanation of existence.

Locke convinced many, if not most, of his contemporaries among the intellectuals of the western world that the human mind discovers the nature of external things exclusively through the senses, and that both the formulation of ideas (the concepts of things) and thought itself were functions of the human reason at work. Individual men would differ in their thinking about the world and man's place in it according to their individual sensory experiences, but all men were endowed with the nervous, psychological, and rational mechanisms for knowing objective reality, for understanding its laws, and for thinking out their own ethical ways of life upon the basis of their individual sensory experiences. Locke's empirical epistemology provided not only a logical basis for a faith in human reason, but also a rational basis for the acceptance of the principles of intellectual individualism. Locke justified a belief in the existence of God upon the basis of what he thought to be a sort of internal sensory evidence, acquired by what might be called an intuitive sensory perception—a point that was very important to Jonathan Edwards in America. In general, however, Locke's explanation of how men know was entirely secular and, for him and his contemporaries, entirely scientific.

It was probably inevitable that, given the nature of the sociological experiences of the American colonial societies, the implications of the Newtonian-Lockean synthesis should have been a powerful determinant in the formulation of American thought in all its aspects, whether economic, social, political, religious, or intellectual. Certainly it had a profound influence upon the formulation of the philosophies of American intellectuals throughout the eighteenth century. It provided a systematic intellectual counterpart to the peculiar experiential challenges of the American adventure that were also a decisive factor in the growth of American philosophies. The results, in the history of philosophy, while they were in most cases adaptations of European ideas, were the formulations of certain American philosophical statements that had no precise counterparts in Europe.

**The Philosophy of Deism.**     As the rigors of life in a stern wilderness softened, and as the implications of the new science made themselves felt in American religious and intellectual circles, the inflexible logic of the Puritan philosophy was subjected to a variety of critical attacks. American preachers like Charles Chauncy and Jonathan Mayhew raised a series of devastating questions relative to the religious and ethical positions of Puritanism, as we saw in Chapter 5. Others, influenced by the implications of the scientific, or "Newtonian," concept of natural law in the universe, rejected or substantially qualified the Puritan concept of a personal creator and governor of the universe whose purposes and whose judgments were both inscrutable and unpredictable (and therefore, in the last analysis and despite the oft-reiterated doctrine of "God's eternal decrees," not very reliable) and substituted for the rule of a divine and somewhat capricious personality that of a system of inflexible and inviolable, and therefore dependable, natural laws. To be sure, God had created the universe and the laws under which it operated. But the great "watchmaker" had then withdrawn and left his great mechanical invention, including man, to function according to its own internal structure and functional potential.

This philosophy, then, was still dualistic, in that it recognized (if not always explicitly) two sorts of reality, the spiritual, which is God, and in which man vaguely shares, and the material. But it was in the material universe that these men, of whom Cadwallader Colden was the most outstanding example in the generation preceding that of the American Revolution, were chiefly interested. Their philosophy, therefore, was in large measure materialistic. The universe they knew was the materialistic universe; man was a rational member of the material universe; his ethical behavior, in his quest for the good life, was to be determined by his own mind; man, directed by his own rational, "enlightened self-interest," was in large measure the master of his own destiny. It was an optimistic philosophy. It was among such men as the Deists that there was formulated (it had often been only assumed) the eighteenth-century doctrine of "progress"; it was largely these men who, by their faith in human reason, gave the mood of their century its customary name of "the Enlightenment."

The starting point of Colden's philosophy was the Newtonian concept of matter and the Lockean explanation of how men know. "Our knowledge of the powers in nature," he wrote, "can only be attained by an accurate observation of the phenomena or effects produced by them and from thence collecting the general rules or laws which these powers observe in producing their effects in different circumstances. We thereby have obtained all the knowledge of nature which can be obtained by our faculties." Within these limits, he believed, it could be observed scientifically that the forces of nature produce three types of action: the "resisting" action of inert matter; the "moving" action observable in such material phenomena as a falling stone or a circulating planet; and "elastic" action, or the capacity to communicate action from one body to another, as in the case of the "aether" that was supposed to pervade the universe. It was to these three that he added, after a correspondence with the idealist Samuel Johnson, a fourth principle of action, which he called "intelligence"; it is this principle that is "the guiding principle in morality, policy, and religion." "It follows, then, that the first formation of all kinds of material systems, the greatest and the least, was made by some intelligent being. . . ." (*See Reading No. 22.*)

Colden was thus forced into a recognition of a universal intelligence. In its operation in living matter, this intelligence appeared to be a sort of "intuitive motion" or "fermentation," inherent in matter itself, which he suggested might be a form of intelligence corresponding, in an elemental way, to the intelligence in men. He never clarified his concept of the "intelligent being" that created the universe; his interest was almost exclusively centered in the nature and the behavior of matter itself. Thus

Colden, while, strictly speaking, he should be called a Deist in his philosophy because of his admission of the logical necessity of a creator, was basically and primarily a materialist in his philosophical interpretation of reality. As such, he anticipated one of the important later strains in American philosophy.

**Idealism in America.** If one of the logical extremes to which the implications of Locke's empiricism might lead was a thorough-going materialism, the opposite extreme was a thorough-going idealism. Thus, if all knowledge, all ideas, and all thought are derived from the impressions of the outside world reported by the nerve-endings of the senses of taste, smell, touch, hearing, and sight, all knowledge of objective reality was internal to the human mind (including the senses). All of the ideas of external things were thus internal, or subjective; all knowledge of, or thought about, the outside world was entirely within the human being. Since one could never be sure whether what the senses reported was really true or not, the Lockean epistemology might lead to a complete logical skepticism as to the validity of human knowledge in its entirety (as it actually did in the philosophy of the great English savant David Hume). On the other hand, it might lead to the conclusion that all reality, in the last analysis, was ideal (that is, pure idea) and that objective reality, in the popular sense of the word, did not exist at all unless perceived by some human mind. This was the position arrived at by the great Anglo-Irish philosopher, Bishop George Berkeley. This was also the position reached by one of the most distinguished American philosophers of the eighteenth century, Samuel Johnson, who became president of King's College in New York. Jonathan Edwards also may be called an idealist in his philosophy because, although he recognized the reality of the matter of the universe, he thought of all things as emanations of the mind of God. Johnson arrived at his philosophical idealism by reading Locke and Berkeley; Edwards arrived at his independently, after a reading of Locke as a boy at Yale.

Johnson closely followed Berkeley in his logical idealism. The true reality, according to his thinking, is the perceptions of things by the mind. (*See Reading No. 23.*) Nothing exists except when perceived by the mind, through the senses. Our minds, he said (following Locke), are *tabulae rasae,* or blank tablets, upon which are engraved the images of things external to ourselves, reported by the senses. But these external things that we perceive are really—and only—reflections of the universal ideas or "archetypes" of things in the mind of God. Thus, the contact of our minds with external things is really a contact with the universal mind of God. Thus, too, all existence external to ourselves is real; but it is a reality of ideas—of mind (that is, of God's mind). The reality in our minds corresponds with, and is dependent upon, the external reality that is the universal mind of God.

The Berkeleian logic followed by Johnson led straight to the conclusion that nothing exists that is not perceived by the mind—and, since the mind is free to choose among the ideas that seem to promise the best road toward the good life, this way of thinking implied a freedom of the will in the resolution of ethical problems or in the choice of a mode of conduct.

On both these major points Jonathan Edwards differed widely from Berkeley, whose work he apparently never read. Coming to his own philosophy directly from his reading of Locke and his observation of existence, Edwards never doubted the objective, concrete reality of the world reported by the senses: "Things," he said, "are what they seem to be." But his thinking did parallel that of Berkeley and Johnson insofar as he accepted the fundamental position of Locke's thought, that the human being's comprehension of external reality was entirely subjective (that is, internal to the human mind) and that the universe, in its entirety and in its concrete reality—or "resistance," as he put it—is a tangible manifestation of the mind of God. Dominated and driven as he was by his concern for practical religion, what difference does it make, he asked, whether things exist only as pure idea or as concrete material substance? The real problem is the problem of knowing that the true ideas in our minds are reflections of ideas in the mind of God, and that we should behave accordingly. The perception of God's beauty, however, is not a function of the rational senses, which acquaint us with objective reality; this perception is a function of the "sense of the heart."

It was this "sense of the heart" that really concerned Edwards. For it was this sense that informed mankind, not only of God's beauty and majesty, but of men's utter dependence upon him. Edwards thus really built his system of philosophy and religion and ethics around his own Puritanical enlargement of Locke's description of the way in which the mind perceives God. (*See Reading No. 24.*)

Edwards' philosophy was probably the most extraordinary intellectual achievement of eighteenth-century America. As a restatement of Calvinism in terms of the Newtonian-Lockean synthesis, it was a spectacular logical success. But as an effort to save Calvinism against the attacks of eighteenth-century "Arminianism," it was a failure. Indeed, the Puritan fathers themselves would probably have disowned him no less for his idealism (as against their dualistic Platonism) than his own generation did reject him because of his stubborn denial of the eighteenth-century rationalists' own dualism of a Newtonian-Lockean material universe and a God who was spirit, with man, uniquely endowed with "reason," participating in the nature of both. It was they who were moving with the march of time, not he. Yet Edwards was the greatest, and probably the most original, of the American philosophers of the eighteenth century. While he failed in his effort to revive a dying Puritanism, yet his influence upon subsequent American philosophy, particularly the transcendentalism of the nineteenth-century, was enormous.

**The Origins of American Pragmatism.**  In the history of philosophy, pragmatism has been rather a theory of knowledge, an epistemology, an explanation and a test of how men know, than a philosophy in the true sense of the word—that is, a systematic explanation of the nature of reality itself. Its central tenet has been that that knowledge is true that is provable by its external effects. Thus, the pragmatic test of religion, for American religious leaders of the eighteenth century such as Cotton Mather, was its effects on the behavior of men.

But the pragmatic attitude, when followed in the secular interests and activities of men, applies this test to every scrap of "knowledge" in the human mind. If the idea of vaccination, applied in medical practice, actually kills bacteria and saves the lives of men, that idea, that knowledge, is demonstrated to be true. If the idea, or "knowledge," that sickness may be cured by incantations over the ill, applied in practice, does not actually cure the sick, the idea is error; the "knowledge" is false. Indeed, it is not knowledge at all, but superstition.

There was a great deal of this hard-headed mood toward knowledge in the thinking of eighteenth-century Americans. There was much of it in the sermons of the preachers, especially those of such "rationalists" as Chauncy and Mayhew; and it affected their religious outlook. There was also much of it—mixed, be it remembered, with much that was sheer superstition—in the folk culture of the farmers and the frontiersmen. The spread of science and the experimental method of investigation contributed to it; there was much of it, also, in the economic and social moods of the people.

Among articulate philosophers it did not achieve, in the colonial period, any formal, systematic presentation. But the pragmatic test was applied to knowledge, to institutions, to religion, even to philosophy itself, by certain hard-headed American intellectuals, the most articulate and the most advanced of whom, on these points, was Benjamin Franklin. (*See Reading No. 25.*)

Franklin retained his clearly pragmatic attitude toward human thought and knowledge throughout his life. One of the major characteristics of his career, indeed, is the way in which, time and again, he proved the validity of an idea or a fund of knowledge by an invention based upon it. The knowledge he acquired by the study of optics, for example, led to his invention of bifocal spectacles; what he learned in his studies of heat eventuated in the so-called "Franklin Fireplace"; his knowledge of electricity and lightning proved itself in the lightning rod. This was knowledge demonstrating its truth and its validity by its pragmatic results.

As has already been suggested, early American pragmatism was more of a mood than a clearly-articulated theory, more of a folk attitude than a philosophy. Yet this mood was widespread among the people. Its influence may be seen, for example, in the rapidly spreading educational interest in new school and college subjects of a pragmatic sort. (*See Chapter 8.*) It may be seen in the shifting emphases in religion; it may also be seen in the new, critical moods in literature. Formal philosophy, whether Puritanism, idealism, or deism, was for the philosophers; pragmatism was a philosophical mood that the people in society at large, without being "philosophers," could understand and share. It might, perhaps, not be too much to say that pragmatism came closer to expressing the mood of American society as a whole toward its experience in the new world than any other form of philosophical thought.

**The Philosophy of "Common Sense."** Puritanism, deism, idealism, and a rudimentary pragmatism were all important currents in the philosophical thinking of the Angloamericans of the colonial period, and all these were of continuing importance in the later development of American thought. It must be remembered, however, that for the vast majority of Americans the basic philosophical (and religious) position was that of "Common Sense," represented by such a philosopher as President John Witherspoon of Princeton, who taught that, after all, existence is of two kinds, matter and spirit. Both kinds were created by God. Men know the truth about matter through their senses; they know the truth about spiritual matters through the intuition of the soul. This was the simple, unlabored philosophy of most Americans, both then and later.

# 7

# ORIGINS OF AMERICAN LITERARY THOUGHT

Any discussion of literature as an element in the history of thought must consider the theme with two of its aspects clearly in mind. One of these is the study of literature as a vehicle of thought, whether comments on human nature, thoughts about religion, mystical or poetic reflections on human experience, pleas for causes, or any other sort of commentary upon the human drama. The other is thought about literature, or literary criticism—discussions of style, thoughts on the use of grammar, literary forms for the expression of ideas, and so on. It is the origins of these two sorts of literary thought that in America interest us here.

**"English" Literature in the Colonies.** The literary product of the English colonies in the seventeenth century was in very large measure (but not entirely) composed of writings by men who were actually Englishmen living in America, or their sons. The thoughts contained in their writings were predominantly the thoughts of Englishmen commenting upon what was happening in the colonies.

The literary pieces that derived from the southern colonies, from John Smith's *Historie of Virginia* onward, were nearly all of this sort. George Hammond's *Leah and Rachel* was a description of the two Chesapeake colonies. George Alsop's *A Character of the Province of Maryland* was a description of life in that province. Ebenezer Cook's *The Sot-Weed Factor* was a mild satire, in verse, on life in the Chesapeake colonies. The exception to the rule was the small but notable body of papers that arose out of Bacon's Rebellion, as will be noted presently; and a genuine Virginia writer with a clear sense of, and feeling for, the uniqueness of the Virginia colonial experience arose about the turn of the century in the person of Robert Beverley, whose *History of Virginia* was published in 1704.

The publications of the New Englanders were predominantly religious; the vast majority of them were sermons. There were a few poets, but most of their poems, whether by Ann Bradstreet, Edward Wigglesworth, or—the greatest of them all—Edward Taylor, were heavily impregnated with the religious thought of Puritanism.

The literary thought of the southern writers of the century, then, with one notable exception, was that of literary description and social commentary; that of New England literature was the thought of Calvinistic Puritanism in America. New England's Puritan self-consciousness flourished in the *Magnalia Christi Americana* (1702) of Cotton Mather, whose life spanned the fourth quarter of the seventeenth century and the first quarter of the eighteenth. But Mather, like Beverley in Virginia, was a transitional figure. Neither of these men was an "Englishman in America": both were genuinely and self-consciously American, although Mather, in particular, displayed a persistent devotion to the literary ideals of the original Puritan generations.

**The Literature of the Colonial Society: The Provincial Mood.**    There never was a moment, in the early history of the colonies, when there were not some men in every colonial society who were interested in literature, either as reading matter to be enjoyed or as a vehicle for self-expression. Such men were relatively rare in the seventeenth century. As colonial society expanded and became more stable, however, and as wealth and leisure came to be achieved by an increasing number of people during the eighteenth century, American literati became relatively and increasingly numerous.

Most Americans interested in literature looked to England as the chief supplier of literary works and as their chief source of inspiration. They took English literature as their model; most of their writing was derived from this model. They followed English fashions of composition, such as the prose of the *Spectator* of London or the poetry of Alexander Pope. And for subject matter they tended to use English, European, or classical experiences or myths, or they devoted themselves to mystical or esoteric religious themes that bore little or no relationship to daily experience. Of this sort was much of the work, for example, of Mather Byles, religious poet, or Thomas Godfrey, the first American dramatist. Needless to say, in their effort to write imitatively, according to preconceived canons of English literary art, the thought-content of their work was not very substantial.

Of much larger stature were William Byrd II of Virginia and Benjamin Franklin of Philadelphia. Byrd, although born in Virginia, was educated in England; his whole intellectual outlook was conditioned by that experience. Franklin deliberately trained himself to write in what he considered the best English style, taking as his model the *Spectator*. But both of these men, though they wrote in an English idiom, wrote of genuinely American experiences. Byrd's best works dealt with the Virginia frontier; Franklin's highly variegated literary opus was that of a sophisticated American tradesman, merchant, scientist, and philosopher.

**The Appearance of an American Literary Tradition.** American literature, properly called such, was born on the American frontier. It may be said to have appeared for the first time in two bits of writing that grew out of events that occurred in the year 1676. One of these was Mrs. Mary Rowlandson's narrative of her captivity among the Indians in the course of King Philip's war in New England; the other was the corpus of poems and other papers that derived from Bacon's Rebellion in Virginia.

Mrs. Rowlandson's narrative, which has been reprinted many times, is a dramatic relation of her experiences among the Indians, a deeply moving commentary upon a poignant American experience. It is a literary vehicle for American Puritan thought, which never weakens in its sense of man's dependence upon God. At the same time, however, it is a vehicle for some plain-spoken American thoughts about Indians and the relations of the two cultures in general.

The literary offshoot of Bacon's Rebellion, on the other hand, the so-called "Burwell Papers," was entirely secular in mood. The rebellion itself was partly a struggle for power in Virginia politics and partly an expression of the white man's cupidity and his hatred of the Indians. The "Papers" center upon Bacon, the leader, and his untimely death:

> Death why so cruell! What no other way
> To manifest thy spleene, but thus to slay
> Our hope of safety, liberty, our all
> Which, through thy tyranny, with him must fall
> To its late chaos?

As the population of the colonies expanded westward, the contact and conflicts of cultures, the Anglo-Saxon on one side and the Indian and French cultures on the other, came to be the subject matter of the vast bulk of American writing. In this large body of literature appear not only narratives of Indian captivities, which are probably the most characteristic part of it, but also many sermons, missionary relations, descriptions of Indian life and culture, the repetition of Indian myths, and records of "Treaties" (conferences and agreements with the Indians). (*See Reading No. 26.*) This literature, of course, incorporated a great deal of thought about the Indians—the Enlightenment's faith in the capacity of the Indians to absorb the white men's civilization as against the frontiersmen's more realistic conviction that the two cultures could not assimilate and that "the only good Indian was a dead one"; the curious fact of adaptation of white men, women, and children to life among the savages as against the utter failure of all efforts to educate Indian boys at white men's schools; the anthropological interests in the Indians expressed by such students as John Bartram and Cadwallader Colden; the religious missionary interest of such men as Conrad Weiser; and so on.

The literature of the contacts and the rivalries between the Anglo-Saxons and their French and Spanish neighbors is also quite plentiful. Many sermons were preached and printed comparing French and British cultures—to the derogation of the former. There was much of hatred in this literature, as may be seen in the poems of John Maylem. (*See Reading No. 27.*) There are also many poems expressing a British-American war-like fervor, and much literary evidence of a nascent American self-consciousness, as in the writings of Dr. William Douglass, Benjamin Franklin, John Huske, William Livingston, Archibald Kennedy, and others. (*See Chapter 10.*)

Other American experiences, also, were reflected in American literature. Thus, the melting pot is a matter of pride: America is already considered to be a land of escape and refuge from European persecutions. Science and its triumphs enjoyed widespread literary celebration (*see Reading No. 18*): one author celebrated in poetry the inestimable values of printing, while another feared that the concentration of attention upon science must inevitably lead to the death of the *belles lettres*. Moreover, much of the religious literature of the period is suffused with religious nationalism.

Out of all these experiences, but most especially out of the contacts of two dissimilar cultures on the frontiers and the international conflicts with foreign enemies, the Americans were building a mythos of America and a corpus of literary expression that constituted the first fruits of a genuinely American literary experience. In them was the true beginning of the American literary tradition.

**Jonathan Edwards and Benjamin Franklin.** The two greatest Angloamerican literary giants of the colonial period were Jonathan Edwards and Benjamin Franklin, the one a Congregational minister of the Connecticut Valley frontier of New England, the other a man-of-the-world, a printer and businessman of the cultural metropolis of Philadelphia.

Jonathan Edwards has been called one of the four or five greatest literary artists America has produced. And this he certainly was, if by the term is meant an artist who creates, with words and ideas, literary works embodying the profoundest manifestations of the intellectual and emotional experiences of humanity. In many ways Edwards was far ahead of his time. For he understood Newton and Locke as few Americans understood them, and he achieved a literary and philosophical synthesis of their two contributions to science and philosophy upon which he based religious literature whose logical and literary perfection and intellectual stature have few rivals in the whole history of human writing. For sheer literary quality, for example, some of the narratives of personal experiences, whether his own or those of others, that often appear in his writings, achieve excellence. As vehicles of thought, these literary pieces almost always center about religion—the religion of God's love for man. Indeed, it has been said that Edwards, in his effort to rehabilitate Calvinism, brought to that rigid religious system a quality of love that was his own unique contribution.

If Jonathan Edwards, as a literary and religious voice of the New England Puritan frontier, was rejected by his society because he failed to reflect, or even to accept, the sociological and religious moods of his time and place (*see Chapters 4 and 5*), Benjamin Franklin was the epitome of nearly everything that might properly be called American. Shrewd, alert, successful, intelligent, widely read and amazingly well informed on the life of his own times, pragmatic in philosophy and in example, Franklin neither probed as deeply into the subtleties of existence as Edwards nor soared anywhere near so high as he above the marketplace into the realms of metaphysics or of mystery.

Edwards, though he hoped to win the multitude by his writing, reached a highly intellectual, sophisticated audience. Franklin was earthy, realistic, close to the affairs and interests of common men. He realized, of course, the necessity and the effectiveness of a clear, plain prose style; he was a conscious stylist. But he was supremely conscious of the value and effectiveness of language and style that common people could understand and enjoy. For him, language was an instrument, a vehicle of thought whose ultimate end was always to get things done.

Franklin's writing covered practically the whole range of eighteenth-century American interests: religion, politics, sociology, education, science, business and economics, colonial administration, diplomacy, and a host of others. Its forms included essays, poetry, polemics, scientific treatises, aphorisms, "tall tales," and others. Franklin's output was enormous. As a vehicle of contemporary thought, as an interpreter of his society and his world, it is as weighty and imposing as that of Edwards. It was as secular and as pragmatic as Edwards' writings were other-worldly and idealistic. Franklin was a literary voice of his society, as Edwards could never be.

The most famous of Franklin's literary pieces is his

*Autobiography,* which has been reprinted many times. But his literary qualities also appear in his scientific and political essays, in his introductions to his almanac, *Poor Richard,* and in his letters—in fact, in everything that he wrote. He was primarily an essayist; but he was a great humorist, and while he realized his own limitations as a poet and although much of the poetry that he published was borrowed, he himself often wrote poetry. His "I Sing My Plain Country Joan" is a good example:

## SONG

Of their Chloes and Phillisses Poets may prate
  I sing my plain Country Joan
Now twelve Years my Wife, still the Joy of my Life
  Blest Day that I made her my own,
                              My dear Friends
  Blest Day that I made her my own.

### 2

Not a Word of her Face, her Shape, or her Eyes,
  Of Flames or of Darts shall you hear;
Tho' I Beauty admire 'tis Virtue I prize,
  That fades not in seventy Years,
                              My dear Friends
  That fades not in seventy Years,

.     .     .

### 8

Were the fairest young Princess, with Million in Purse
  To be had in Exchange for my Joan,
She could not be a better Wife, mought be a Worse,
  So I'd stick to my Joggy alone
                              My dear Friends
  I'd cling to my lovely ould Joan.

**The Literature of American Self-Consciousness: History.**   One of the most important new forms of literature to appear in Angloamerica during the eighteenth century was history. There had been historical works written during the seventeenth century, to be sure—works by William Bradford, John Winthrop, Captain John Smith, and others. But all these writers were Englishmen, describing the experiences of Englishmen in a new and strange land. The American historians of the eighteenth century, beginning with Robert Beverley and Cotton Mather, were Americans writing of American experiences that they had shared and of American societies of which they were members and whose ideas and ideals they both shared and expressed.

Most of them—Thomas Prince of Massachusetts, Robert Callender of Rhode Island, William Smith of New York, William Stith of Virginia, and Thomas Hutchinson of Massachusetts, for example—wrote of their own colonial societies, each inspired by a desire to present to the world the history and the excellencies of his own society, his "country." William Douglass, alone among them, undertook to write a history of all the colonies (which he never finished). He was particularly interested, as a British nationalist, in the conflict between the English colonies and the French. All of these historians had one thing in common: their self-consciousness about the colonial societies and the differentness of these societies, both from the mother country and from the rest of the world. As a form of literature, their histories were also an important vehicle of a growing American self-consciousness. (*See also Chapter 10.*)

The American colonial histories were the literary mouthpieces of a nascent American self-consciousness, a realization that American society was unique, different from and superior to the other societies of the world. It was not yet nationalism, for none of these historians thought of the colonies as a separate nation. But the colonists did think of their societies as peculiar and especially fortunate segments of the British Empire-nation. The history of their appearance, growth, and peculiar virtues was, for the American historians, matter for profound and devoted historical study.

**The Beginnings of American Literary Criticism.** There was but little literary criticism in seventeenth-century Angloamerica. Some there was, however. Both Robert Beverley and Cotton Mather were conscious of the problem of style, and Mather was quite explicit on the subject. Mather was a self-conscious stylist. Although many of his works were written in a simple, direct style, when he was writing for his own enjoyment or for an arty or literary effect, he appears to have preferred the complex, formal manner, studded with classical references, that his grandson, Rev. Mather Byles, called the "bombastic" or "grubstreet" style. Of his style in the *Magnalia Christi Americana,* Mather says:

> Whereas others, it may be, will reckon the *style* embellished with too much of *ornament,* by the multiplied reference to other and former concerns, closely couched, for the observation of the attentive, in almost every paragraph; but I must confess, that I am of his mind who said, Sienti Sal modici cibis aspersus Condit, et gratiam saporis addit, ita si poulam antiquitatis ad miscueris, Oratio sit venustior [*As a little salt seasons food, and increases its relish, so a spice of antiquity heightens the charm of style*].

Actually, when Mather set out to counsel young ministers on how to preach and write, he advised a simple, understandable style. However, he said,

> If . . . you try your young Wings now and then to see what Flights you can make, at least for an Epigram, it may a little sharpen your Sense, and polish your Style, for more important Performances; . . . . However, since every Man will have his own Style, I would pray, that one may learn to treat one another with mutual Civilities, and Condescensions, and handsomely indulge one another in this, as Gentlemen do in other Matters.

But the fashion in literary style was changing. Mather was practically the last American writer deliberately to write in the old style or to think along these lines in his literary criticism. There was, indeed, a good deal of thought among the Angloamerican writers of the eighteenth century about the use of language as a medium of expression and about the problem of what constituted a good literary style. Franklin was conscious of the problem and deliberately patterned his own literary style after that of the *Spectator,* as we have seen. Mather Byles, the "poet laureate" of eighteenth-century Boston, poked fun at the old, florid style of the writers of the earlier generations—including, apparently, that of his own kinsman, Cotton Mather: "Rattling periods, uncouth jargon, affected phrases and finical jingles—let them be condemned; let them be hissed from the desk and blotted from the page." (*See Reading No. 28.*)

Charles Chauncy felt even more strongly on the subject. He brusquely rejected any conscious effort at style as a matter of art, but went on to analyze the nature and function of language itself. Jonathan Edwards also devoted much profound thought to the nature of language in its relation to the communication of ideas. With these two men, thought about literary expression rose to the level of epistemology.

Literary criticism *per se* was developing rapidly. Cotton Mather had interested himself in the criticism of poetry—and of critics. He recommended "some acquaintance with it" to his young colleagues, and recommended especially Horace, Homer, and Virgil, albeit with a certain sidelong glance at the morals of Homer's gods. Still, he concurred in the critical canon that "it is a false Critic who with a petulant Air, will insult Reason itself, if it presumed to oppose such Authority." On the whole, however, both with Mather and those who followed him, the basic canon of literary criticism was the rule that literature must serve a moral purpose. For example, one of the earliest journalistic critiques of plays in Angloamerica, published in *The American Magazine* in 1758, recognizes many values in "The Story of Ages," the play under discussion (*see Reading No. 29*), and commends especially the moral force of one of the lines, which "reaches at once the understanding and the heart, and was applauded with a zeal that did equal honour to the author, the actor, and the audience."

Literary criticism was concerned with literature as art; it was also concerned (as it has continued to be, in considerable measure, from that day to this) with the ultimate moral qualities and effects of literature. American literature was becoming self-conscious and self-critical. There was little in the accepted canons of literary criticism, of course, that differed from the basic principles of literary criticism of the same period in England. The significant aspect of this earliest literary criticism in America lay in the bald fact of its appearance and in the fact that the elementary canons of literary criticism accepted by the eighteenth-century Americans remained the basic canons of literary criticism until the twentieth.

In the century or so between about 1660 and about 1760, then, the focal emphasis in the subject matter of American literature changed radically. In New England, at least, the literature of the seventeenth century centered about God, and man's relationships to him. In the eighteenth, and increasingly, even in New England, the focus was upon man and his adventures and experiences in this world. This shift of emphasis reflected the shifts in emphasis in thinking upon other aspects of life—political, social, economic, and otherwise. The mood of American literature was of a piece with the over-all mood of the eighteenth-century Enlightenment, but it was also, and clearly, given a special American content and flavor by the peculiarly American frontier experience. The American colonial societies were on the move; they were building themselves, and expanding, at a phenomenal rate. Life here on this earth, on the American frontier or in the zone just back of it, was a great adventure; it was exciting; it was fun; it was interesting; it was the subject matter of the earliest truly American literature.

## — 8 —

# EDUCATION, THE PRESS, AND INTELLECTUAL FREEDOM

### Part 1—Education

Education, in the English society from which the colonial societies sprang, according to Bernard Bailyn, was "largely instinctive and traditional, little articulated and little formalized. . . . Family, community, and church together accounted for the greater part of the mechanism by which English culture transferred itself across the generations." * Yet education was a matter of great importance to the Englishmen who founded the colonies, especially to those who founded New England: Massachusetts, for example, had created a college and a system of primary and secondary schools in the towns within two decades of the colony's founding. Education, however, was hardly self-conscious, or even thought of (except for prospective members of the ministry or the medical or the legal profession) as being differentiated from other normal, automatic social processes. Its objective was the transmission of the intellectual and folkloric *status quo* without change.

In a certain sense, however, there were two English societies that transplanted themselves in America; each had its own idea of what the social and intellectual *status quo* ought to be. One of these was the Anglican, aristocratically inspired society that grew up in the southern colonies and

* Bernard Bailyn, *Education in the Forming of American Society: Needs and Opportunities for Study* (Chapel Hill: The University of North Carolina Press, 1960), pp. 15, 18-19.

72

the British islands of the Caribbean; the other was the Puritan-dissenter, middle-class-minded society that established itself in the colonies of New England. Toward the end of the seventeenth century, a third subdivision of English society, the Quakers, took the initiative in founding the colonial society of Pennsylvania. Each of these three major sociological groups had its own ideas as to what education for the perpetuation of its peculiar concept of the *status quo* ought to be.

The leaders of the Englishmen who first went to the southern colonies, who were predominantly Anglican in religion, brought with them the attitude that was current among the English gentry of that time. Thus Governor Sir William Berkeley of Virginia, when asked what measures were taken in the Colony for "instructing the people . . . in the Christian religion," replied,

> The same course that is taken in England out[*side*] of towns; every man according to his ability instructing his children. . . . But, I thank God, there are no free schools nor printing [*in Virginia*], and I hope we shall not have these hundred years; for learning has brought disobedience, and heresy, and sects into the world, and printing has divulged them, and libels against the best government. God keep us from both!

Education, thus, was thought of as a private affair; it was something for the upper classes, the leaders of society, not for the common people. The education of the children in a family was assumed to be the responsibility of the father; the chief goal of education was the renaissance objective of producing a cultivated gentleman. While this aim was in general a secular one, it included a recognition of the need for at least a modicum of instruction in the tenets of the Anglican religion. For religion, especially the Anglican religion, was also one of the functions of society; the aristocratic social outlook was bound up with both religion and education in the saying that a man might be a Christian in any church, but that, to be a gentleman, he must be an Anglican!

These traditional English ideas with regard to education naturally inclined the settlers in Virginia toward making education a private enterprise, conducted by tutors or small private schools. This tendency was accentuated by the rise of the plantation system of agriculture and the geographical distribution of Virginia society. For where the separate families of plantation owners lived at considerable distances —often, miles—from each other, it was practically impossible to have schools that any considerable number of children could attend.

The leaders of the Puritan migration were highly educated men. Their social and religious ideas derived from the English middle class and accentuated the belief in the necessity of a certain amount of education for all the members of society. True to their dependence upon the Bible as the sole source of religious truth and guidance, they were convinced that every person in the community must be able to read Holy Writ. Therefore, schools were to be made available to everyone; it was the responsibility of the community, acting through the town or the provincial government, to provide them. It was on the basis of thinking such as this that Massachusetts passed the educational laws of 1642 and 1647, which required the towns not only to provide schools, but also to support them.

The interest in producing literate Christians was not the only motive dictating Puritan thinking about education, however. For, in a more general way, the Puritans were sufficiently children of the Renaissance to have a strong belief that knowledge and a trained mind were closer to the virtuous life than was ignorance. It was one of the systematic purposes of "that old deluder Satan" to keep men in ignorance; if the ideals of the Puritan utopia were to be realized, the designs of the old deluder in this respect must be defeated. Furthermore, the utopian Puritan society must have trained leaders, whether religious or secular. Therefore, a college must be established to train them. It was for this reason that the Massachusetts Assembly passed an ordinance in 1636 providing for the establishment of a college, which, because of the munificent bequest of John Harvard, was named Harvard College.

The Quakers who founded Pennsylvania, true to their religious principle of the "inner voice," held that true wisdom is the wisdom of the heart, in its communion with God; this wisdom was not to be learned in school. Yet the Quakers and other pietists of the middle colonies did have educational ideas of a very clear sort. These ideas centered about the conviction that children should be taught useful occupations. Thus while book learning received an adequate minimum of attention, instruction of a utilitarian sort was provided, in one way or another, for practically every child. Such schools as existed were parochial schools, maintained by local Friends' "meetings" or other pietistic religious groups.

If the Quakers and the German pietists were distrustful of much book learning, the non-Quaker, non-pietist inhabitants of the middle colonies were not. The Anglicans in New York, New Jersey, and Pennsylvania—and they constituted, probably, the most numerous separate groups in these colonies—of course shared the gentlemanly educational ideals of their co-religionists to the southward. Society in New York and New Jersey and, to a lesser degree, perhaps, in Pennsylvania, early took on a distinctly aristocratic caste; the educational thinking of the Anglicans here followed aristocratic theory and practice, along lines similar to those in Virginia, Maryland, and South Carolina. The fact that society in the middle colonies was largely urban, however, was of considerable importance in the development of education in all of them.

**Education for a Society in the Process of Change.** During the two or three generations that followed the successful establishment of the colonial societies, those original societies passed through a complex set of profound and rapid changes. The basic economic and social patterns laid down in the seventeenth century remained, to be sure, as they would for another century or more; but the societies themselves all enjoyed a phenomenal expansion. The areas of improved land spread out; the frontier zone moved steadily westward; the numbers of the population were multiplied, both by natural increase and by immigration; the patterns of life and culture became more complex and more modern with the admixture of foreign cultures, the wide circulation of newspapers, and, most of all, the infiltration into the colonist's intellectual life of the findings and the implications of science.

As was true in the evolution of religion, there were several profound sociological factors at work making for change in American educational thought. The first of these was the immigration of many non-English persons and groups to make Angloamerican society a highly cosmopolitan one, with a consequent diversification of educational thinking. The second was the frontier, with its emphasis upon adaptability, its egalitarianism, and its premium upon inventiveness. The third was science and its assumption of the rationality and the educability of the human mind. American society was in the process of growth; high premiums were placed upon individual initiative, inventiveness, originality of thought. Education, reflecting all these, ceased to be an "instinctive and traditional" social function for the perpetuation of the *status quo* and became a conscious, specialized instrument for the pragmatic and progressive purposes of a society in the midst of rapid evolution. The individual was not now to be inducted into a static social and intellectual *milieu:* he was to be prepared to adapt himself to, and take advantage of, the new circumstances developing about him.

Benjamin Franklin was the most significant of eighteenth-century Angloamerican educational thinkers. Franklin's most famous writings on education were his *Proposals Relating to the Education of Youth in Pennsylvania,* published in 1749 (*see Reading No. 30*), and his *Idea of the English School,* published in 1751. In preparing these, he read many European books on education by such advanced thinkers as John Locke, George Turnbull, Charles Rollin, and others, and from them he borrowed many ideas; but the resulting synthesis and its American application are distinctly his own, directed toward the problems of education that were peculiar to America. He expressed this idea in the preface to *The American Instructor* (1748), which was a sort of Franklin-revised edition of George Fisher's *The Instructor: or Young Man's Best Companion,* published in London: "In the British Edition of this Book, there were many things of little or no Use in these Parts of the World: In this Edition those things are omitted, and in their Room many other Matters inserted, more immediately useful to us Americans." As for the need for a general education, he said, "For though the American Youth are allow'd not to want Capacity; yet the best Capacities require Cultivation, it being truly with them, as with the best Ground, which unless well tilled and sowed with profitable Seed, produces only ranker Weeds."

It is clear that it was the pragmatic side of his program that lay uppermost in Franklin's mind. The students were to be prepared to take advantage of the practical occasions that would present themselves in life. "Thus instructed," he said, "youth will come out of this [*the English*] school fitted for learning any business, calling, or profession."

The Reverend William Smith proposed a program quite similar to that of Franklin, in *A General Idea of the College of Mirania,* published in 1754. As a result he was elected to be the first Rector of the Philadelphia Academy. In his educational practice he turned out to be somewhat more conservative than he was in his theories, but he did exercise a vigorous liberal influence in the conscious expansion of the educational and cultural life of Philadelphia.

Others shared this more pragmatic, "open-ended" thinking about education. Hugh Jones, in Virginia, declared that youth should be taught the English language; any other was useless and a waste of time. Cadwallader Colden gave enthusiastic endorsement to Franklin's educational proposals and added an emphasis of his own upon the necessity of cultivating the civic virtues: "I think," he said, "the Power of a Nation consists in the knowledge and Virtue of its inhabitants. . . ." This emphasis upon civic virtue was a widespread characteristic of American educational thinking. Thus, Archibald Kennedy of New York recognized both the civic values of education and the liberal, fluid nature of American society when he wrote that

The Intention and Design of Seminaries, in every Country governed by Laws, are to form the Minds of Youth, to Virtue, and to make them useful Members of the Society, in whatever Station may be allotted to them, in Conformity to the Law of the Land. . . . In Countries, where Liberty prevails, and where the Road is left open for the Son of the meanest Plebeian, to arrive at the highest Pitch of Honors and Preferments, there never will be wanting great Emulation, and of Course great Men.

**The Conservative Mood in Education.** For all these liberal thinkers, American society was an "open society." The chief objective of education was the preparation of the individual for life in such a society.

There was, of course, a strong and persistent current

of conservative thought in the field of education that sought to preserve the old values of the traditional educational way against the popular, secular, and pragmatic tendencies of the liberal innovations. Usually, the conservative mood was strongest among the aristocratic classes and the clergy —those who had the most to gain or preserve—by the maintenance of the *status quo* against the liberal tide. For them, the chief object of education was still the cultivation of the "gentleman," as distinguished from "the common sort"—the man of culture and virtue, with a mind trained to think and to assume the responsibilities of government that fell upon the shoulders of the upper stratum of the stratified society. These qualities were to be cultivated by a study of the classical languages, reading of the classical books, and, most of all, a rigorous training in Aristotelian logic. In its essence, this sort of thinking was essentially medieval; but it was reasserted in America with an emphasis added by the challenge of the new American circumstances.

Perhaps the clearest and most concise statement of the conservative stake in education was a remark by Cadwallader Colden, conservative member of the conservative "court party" in New York, who, although he had endorsed Franklin's proposals for an Academy, lamented the dominance of the dissenters in the field of education and recommended the establishment of "a seminary on the principles of the Church of England [*to*] be distinguished in America by particular privilege, not only on account of religion, but of good policy, to prevent the further growth of republican principles, which already too much prevail in the colonies." Colden accepted the idea that education was a self-conscious instrument of social policy. As a conservative, he feared the rapid growth of "republicanism," which was being spread, in his opinion, by the schools of the dissenters. His proposal was for an Anglican institution "distinguished in America by special privileges" to train up a class of civic leaders who might be depended upon to maintain the tried-and-true social and political system of the England that he took as his model.

The conservative attitude in educational thought was able to retard the innovations proposed by Franklin and his fellow liberals. Practice lagged somewhat behind thought.

Yet both thought and practice in education were changing. Education in the colonies, as of about 1760, was far more secular in outlook, more pragmatic, more fluid, more calculated to encourage individual originality and dissent from authority than it had been in the year 1660. As an event in the history of educational thought, the changes in American experience expressed themselves in educational ideas: it is in these new ideas—both the liberal and the conservative ones—that are to be found the origins of the thinking and the practices that have come to characterize American educational thought of a later day.

## Part 2—The Press

Closely related to education as a vehicle of intellectual life in early America was the press. The term includes, of course, books, pamphlets, sermons, almanacs, and broadsides, as well as newspapers and magazines. All these sorts of printed matter except the last circulated widely; all served educational and informational ends. It is probable that printed sermons and almanacs were read by more people than any other form of reading matter in the first half of the eighteenth century; but newspapers, after the founding of the first fairly successful newspaper in 1704, reached a number of readers that increased rapidly and steadily throughout the eighteenth century.

**The English Heritage.**   There was, in fact, very little printing of any kind in Angloamerica in the seventeenth century. The first press had been inaugurated at Cambridge, Massachusetts, in 1638, and this press alone, among the printing ventures of the century, enjoyed an active and relatively distinguished career. Governor William Berkeley, as we have seen, thanked God there was no printing press in Virginia. William Nuthead did open a press at Jamestown in 1682, only to have it suppressed a few months later by royal order for publishing certain documents without prior permission. William Bradford opened a press at Philadelphia in 1685, but presently moved to New York in search of a more congenial climate for his product. Richard Pierce and Benjamin Harris published one issue of their first American newspaper, *Public Occurrences,* at Boston in September of 1690, only to have it promptly suppressed by the Governor and Council. Even as late as 1727, James

Franklin abandoned his *New England Courant* under the pressure of censorship by the Governor and Council of Massachusetts and moved to Newport, Rhode Island, to found the *Rhode Island Gazette*; James' apprentice, his younger brother Benjamin, had long since sought a more liberal *milieu* in Philadelphia.

The press, such as was permitted to exist in the seventeenth century, was considered to be a mere mechanical tool of the state or the established church. Its function was to publish such materials as the state or the church saw fit to publish, in the interest of maintaining the *status quo*. In 1662 the colony of Massachusetts enacted a law requiring that the manuscript of every proposed publication be submitted to the official board of censors for approval before printing. Under this regime, publication of *The Imitation of Christ* was held up until certain papistical passages were excised! Colonial governors were regularly instructed "to provide that noe person have any press for printing, nor that any book, or other matters whatsoever be printed without . . . especial leave to license first obtained."

The practical needs of the community, nevertheless, forced upon it an acceptance of printing establishments, especially after the turn of the century. The first regular newspaper, *The Boston News-Letter*, was started in 1704. In the half-century that followed, newspapers began to be published in nearly all the colonies; in some of them, by 1760, there were several newspapers.

**The Function of the Press in an Open Society.** The intellectual climate was changing. As early as 1696 a jury in Salem, Massachusetts, defied the presiding judge and declared Thomas Maule not guilty of libel for publishing facts. At the same time it asserted the revolutionary doctrine that publishing the facts was not necessarily libel and that the printer had a right to publish them. The jury in the famous case of John Peter Zenger, in New York (1734), did the same thing. Zenger's counsel, Andrew Hamilton of Pennsylvania, after a most eloquent assertion of the intellectual validity and the social utility of the liberty of the press, was given a popular ovation and the freedom of the city of New York in recognition of his "learned and generous defence of the rights of mankind, and the liberty of mankind, and the liberty of the press." (*See Reading No. 31.*)

Many other statements and defenses of the principles of the liberty of publication, whether in newspapers or books or elsewhere, found expression in Angloamerica in the eighteenth century; and the Continental Congress was engaging in no idle talk, in its address to the Canadians in 1774, when it pointed to freedom of the press as one of the most sacred rights of Americans and proclaimed the thirteen colonies to be the most liberal society in the world in this regard.

The acquittal of Zenger on the basis of Hamilton's plea was exceptional for the time and probably had no significant immediate effect upon licensing laws or other forms of censorship—or, for that matter, upon the procedures of the courts in such cases. The significance of this case lies in the clear and dramatic way in which it shows how the ideas of the freedom of the press that have been so important in American history, ideas shared by Franklin and many other liberal thinkers of the time, had their beginnings.

That it did affect other thinkers is shown by a series of essays attributed to William Livingston of New York, which was published in the *Independent Reflector* in 1753. (*See Reading No. 32.*) These later articles, however, while clear and unequivocal on the desirability and public utility of freedom of the press, gave somewhat more emphasis to the idea that with freedom goes responsibility. They emphasized the principle that the press, if it is to enjoy freedom, must also discipline itself and operate with honesty and integrity.

Actually, it was still a long time before the American press achieved complete freedom of publication, even after the American Revolution. But the origins of American liberal thought on the subject are to be found among the outstanding American publicists and lawyers of the eighteenth century, origins derived partly from ideas received from contemporary liberal thinkers in England and partly from convictions born of such everyday practical political experiences as the personal experiences of Benjamin Franklin or the conflict between Governor Cosby and the New York Assembly that had brought fame to Peter Zenger.

## Part 3—Thought on Intellectual Freedom

The earliest English colonies in America were not founded as havens of intellectual or religious freedom. Neither of these ideas, indeed, was characteristic of the culture of the first half of the seventeenth century, either in England or in America. Rhode Island and, in a degree, Maryland were, as we have seen, the only exceptions to the rule, so far as religion was concerned. The idea of intellectual freedom in general—of complete freedom of inquiry and of expression—had only just appeared, in the writings of a very few Europeans, at the moment, say, when the *Mayflower* put out to sea. The appearance of this idea in Europe and its origins and development in America were events of the late seventeenth century in England and of the eighteenth in America.

**Intellectual Freedom and Social Change.** We have already considered, in Chapter 4, the origins and the growth of the idea of freedom of religious thought. At what point did the secular aspect of freedom of thought, or the idea of intellectual freedom in general, appear? The idea seems to have appeared in America in two areas of thought almost simultaneously, in the course of political debate and in the course of the spread of science.

In the area of political debate, for example, many men went so far as to espouse not only the doctrines of criticism of and resistance to the government, but even the doctrine of the right of revolution. And if men were thinking along such lines, they obviously considered themselves free to do so; and they explicitly demanded that freedom. This meant, in effect, that they demanded—or assumed—the freedom both to think radical thoughts and to communicate those thoughts to others. It is probably true, as Clifford Shipton says, that the generally antimonarchical tone of Jonathan Mayhew's sermon on the death of King George II of England "would have sent the preacher to the scaffold for treason in another nation." * And Benjamin Franklin,

* Clifford K. Shipton, editor, *Biographical Sketches of Those Who Attended Harvard College in the Classes 1741-1745. Sibley's Harvard Graduates,* Volume XI, 1741-1745 (Boston: Massachusetts Historical Society, 1960), p. 463.

writing to Cadwallader Colden, frankly recognized that "It is well we are not, as poor Galileo was, subject to the Inquisition for philosophical heresy. My whispers against the orthodox doctrine, in private letters, would be dangerous; but your writing and printing would be highly criminal. As it is, you must expect some censure; but one heretic will surely excuse another." Americans were conscious of the fact that in the British Empire, and especially in their part of it, there was a greater degree of freedom of expression than in any other society in the world. Mayhew himself, in the preface to that famous sermon of 1750 on unlimited submission, gloried in this fact:

> GOD be thanked, one may, in any part of the *British* dominions, speak freely (if a decent regard be paid to those in authority) both of government and religion; and even give some broad hints, that he is engaged on the side of Liberty, the BIBLE and Common Sense, in opposition to Tyranny, PRIEST-CRAFT and Nonsense, without being in danger either of the *Bastile* or the *Inquisition*.

Meanwhile, the correspondence among eighteenth-century scientists is full of exchanges of their findings. They keenly felt the need for learning from each other and for some systematic medium or institution for the exchange of ideas. It was out of this need that the scientific societies, such as the American Philosophical Society, arose. And it was out of this experience that American intellectuals came to realize the utility of and the philosophical justification for complete freedom of scientific inquiry and of expression.

Jonathan Mayhew was clear and unequivocal in his espousal of the idea of intellectual freedom:

> Free examination, weighing arguments for and against, with impartiality, is the way to find the truth. Who imagines that free inquiry into philosophical [*i.e., scientific*] subjects has any tendency to lead men into a wrong idea of the natural world? . . . Error and ignorance fly from the light, like the owl and bat; but truth and honesty, like the noble eagle, face to the sun. . . . This right was given them by God, and nature, and the gospel of Christ; and no man has a right to deprive another of it, under a notion that he will make an ill use of it, and fall into erroneous opinions.

This ideal of intellectual freedom and the faith in progress by the free exchange of ideas was eloquently expressed on various occasions by John Randolph, Speaker of the Virginia House of Burgesses. Randolph's interest in the freedom of speech was directed chiefly at the freedom of the representatives of the people in their legislature to speak without restraint on any subject, but the principle had a much broader application and was echoed in many other areas by many voices. For the House of Burgesses, said Randolph, "Freedom of Speech is the very Essence of their Being. . . ." (*See Reading No. 33.*)

**Conservative and Religious Resistance.** In practice, the idea of intellectual freedom had to fight an uphill battle. We have already seen the resistance, religious and even scientific, to the practice of inoculation. And when Doctor William Shippen carried his study of anatomy to the point of dissecting corpses, his laboratory was destroyed by a mob: what he was doing was thought to be destroying the chances of those persons whose corpses he was cutting to pieces from appearing before God on the day of judgment. Similarly, intellectual conservatives feared the effect of complete intellectual freedom upon both religion and popular behavior. Yet the winds of intellectual freedom, the breath of the eighteenth-century Enlightenment in America, were blowing. And Benjamin Franklin probably expressed the dominant mood of many of the intellectual leaders of eighteenth-century Angloamerica when he reprinted, in his brother's newspaper, this passage from *Cato's Letters*:

Without Freedom of Thought, there can be no such thing as Wisdom; and no such thing as publick Liberty, without Freedom of Speech; which is the Right of every Man, so far as by it, he does not hurt or controul the Right of another: And this is the only Check it ought to suffer, and the only Bounds it ought to know.

The thinking of many of the intellectual leaders of American colonial society with regard to education, the press, and intellectual freedom in general was evidently moving in a liberal direction, toward a greater freedom and an education for freedom in all these areas. To be sure, there were conservative reactions and conservative thinking as well. But the evidence seems clear that "liberty," a word almost universally used among Americans, really meant individual freedom and that this devotion to "liberty" was based upon a well-nigh universal conviction that individual intellectual freedom, up to the point where it might infringe upon the "liberty" of another, was the true basis and effective mechanism for the achievement of individual self-improvement and social and political progress.

## — 9 —

# ORIGINS OF AMERICAN VIEWS
# ON INTERNATIONAL AFFAIRS

The colonization of the American hemisphere by Europeans marked the opening of a new era in the history of the world community of nations. For from this colonization there grew a group of new nations whose interests and whose voices would one day come to be of great importance in the determination of the world community's affairs. From the very beginning of European overseas colonization, the rivalries of the European states for the possession of the American continent, for commerce with it, and for the rights of their respective citizens in the "New World" added a congeries of new issues to the nexus of international diplomacy. At the same time, the European colonies themselves discovered that their own self-interests were affected in new and varied ways by the local circumstances in which they found themselves. These local circumstances led them into attitudes and policies, in their external relations, that often differed substantially from those of their mother countries. The English colonies in America were no exception. Out of the peculiar local and continental circumstances of their existence and their experience, there arose certain basic needs, different from those of England, that expressed themselves in attitudes and policies that were to characterize American external relations for several centuries.

Naturally enough, most American thinking about international affairs focused upon the international situation in the American hemisphere, since it was here that international affairs affected them most closely. Thus, although there was no end of accurate information published in their papers about international affairs in Europe, and although the Americans were vitally interested in European diplomatic affairs, it was almost exclusively about their own international contacts and interests that they expressed opinions of their own. When they did express themselves, their opinions were clear and decisive.

**The English Connection.**    All of the men and women who first peopled the English colonies in America were Englishmen. And as the era in which the colonies were founded was that marked by the tensions and warfare of the first half of the seventeenth century, their attitudes toward the other nations of the world were those of any other Englishmen. They were directly concerned with English international policies and relations, since they were exposed to attack both by European fleets and armies and by their non-English neighbors in America. It behooved them to be both informed and alert. Furthermore, insofar as they were involved in international affairs, those affairs were negotiated for them by the English ministers. Although the colonists had little voice in the formulation of British diplomatic policies, they were bound to be interested in such policies, since their very survival might depend upon them. The time was to come, indeed, when the colonies would consciously attempt to influence the conduct of British foreign relations with regard to them.

In general, the thinking of European diplomats of the seventeenth and eighteenth centuries was a mixture of mercantilistic ideas and dynastic ambitions. In the name of a mythical sort of "balance of power," it sought to reconcile the aggressive imperialisms of their respective states and restrictive limitations upon their neighbors.

Fortunately for the English colonies, England's power was steadily mounting during the eighteenth century. Except for the combined War of Jenkins' Ear and War of the Austrian Succession (1739-1748), which ended in a stalemate, England emerged from every war it fought between 1700 and 1763 with a considerable accretion of colonial territory and commercial power. Thus, the English colonies were preserved from being given to other powers, while solid societies of Swedes, Dutchmen, Spaniards, and

French in America were delivered, body, soul, and property, to England.

Throughout these centuries of European rivalries and wars, the English colonies in America were dependent, for their very existence as English colonies, upon the mother country's military and diplomatic protection. They participated in the mother country's wars; they often gained or lost by the success or failure of the mother country's diplomacy with regard to them. They had, perforce, to be interested.

**Colonial Attitudes Toward International Affairs.**    One of the basic attitudes of Americans toward international affairs was that which rested upon the feeling of escape from the troubles of the old continent and of isolation from European conflict. This feeling manifested itself very early, especially in New England: "There never was a generation," wrote Increase Mather in 1677, "that did so perfectly shake off the dust of Babylon both as to ecclesiastical and civil constitution, as the first generation of Christians that came into this land for the gospel's sake." And Rev. Francis Daniel Pastorius wrote that "after I had sufficiently seen the European provinces and countries, and the threatening movements of war, and had taken to heart the dire changes and disturbances of the Fatherland, I was impelled through a special guidance from the Almighty, to go to Pennsylvania."

Many of the colonial leaders blessed God for the three thousand miles of ocean that separated them from that unhappy continent, Europe, and they early expressed the sentiments that later came to be associated with American isolationism. Thus, Massachusetts in 1652 officially informed the Dutch of New Netherland that the Anglo-Dutch war that began in that year was not of Massachusetts' making, that the colony would have no part in it, and that the merchants of the commonwealth would continue to trade with the Dutch colony as in times of peace. Similarly, the English and French colonists on the island of St. Christopher's in the West Indies made a treaty in 1678 dividing the island between them and agreeing that they would mutually maintain a policy of isolation in the case of conflict between the mother countries in Europe.

Yet the Americans were keenly interested in international affairs, and they realized increasingly, during the eighteenth century, that their peace and their happiness were bound up with the tides of European diplomacy. That they were both interested and well informed with regard to international affairs is demonstrated by the fact that "foreign news" constituted by far the most extensive segment of the content of colonial newspapers. The dispatches from Europe published in the newspapers kept the colonists surprisingly well informed. On the basis of this information, coupled with that in the letters they received from Europe and their analysis of their own situation, colonial thinkers made many penetrating commentaries upon international affairs, usually relating their own international problems to the relationships in the Atlantic community of nations as a whole.

James Logan of Philadelphia, for example, wrote a masterly survey of the international situation in America in 1732. (*See Reading No. 34.*) In this memorial, Logan reiterated an idea that was common on both sides of the Atlantic: that the balance of power in Europe depended upon the balance of colonial possessions. Much of England's power and prosperity, he said, depended upon the wealth that the country derived from its colonies; "the Loss of them to any other Power especially to France might be its own [*England's*] ruin."

This same idea was repeated by Sir William Keith, one-time governor of Pennsylvania, who pleaded with the English government after his return to England, about 1740, not to surrender to Spain any of the land occupied by Georgia or South Carolina north of the St. John's River. It was also reiterated in an English pamphlet reprinted in Boston in 1755, in which the author, one "T.C.," bluntly stated that "the Balance of Power will inevitably fall into the Hands of him who becomes possessed of the Continent of North America, and to whom all the Sugar Islands must fall of course, because they can't subsist without the said Continent."

In all of these statements the Americans were attempting to influence the foreign policy of the mother country, especially with regard to Angloamerica. Such men as William Livingston of New York, Doctor William Douglass, the Reverend Charles Chauncy, Governor William Shirley

of Massachusetts, and others were extremely articulate in
their suggestions offered to the British Ministry. Governor
Shirley was named one of the English Commissioners on
the Anglo-French joint commission that met in Paris in
1750 in an effort to agree upon a definition of the two
nations' colonial possessions in America. As time went on,
the American commentators became more and more bel-
ligerent, more and more imperialistic, more and more inspired by the spirit of "manifest destiny."

**International Thinking Dictated by Experience and
Self-Interest.**    Very soon after their settlement in America,
the colonies had discovered that their relationships with the
non-English parts of the world, particularly those in
America, involved circumstances that were different from
those confronted by the mother country, and that their own
attitudes and policies must of necessity be different from
those of the homeland.

Thus, in the course of their growth and experience the
English colonies engaged in certain direct relations with
their non-English neighbors and formulated certain international policies of their own—policies, be it noted, that
were not always entirely in harmony with those of the
mother country.

These elementary international relations were conducted
by individual colonies. The Colony of Plymouth, in 1627,
made an informal commercial agreement with Dutch New
Netherland; Massachusetts made a similar agreement with
Acadia in 1644, the New England Confederation (in Connecticut) made a boundary agreement with New Netherland in 1650; Virginia negotiated a commercial treaty with
Dutch New Netherland in 1660. In the 1680's Governor
Dongan of New York engaged in a direct correspondence
with the French governor of Canada over the question of
which nation should have suzerainty over the Iroquois
Indians; in 1724 Governor Belcher of Massachusetts engaged in a set of negotiations with the French governor of
Canada over the question of control of the Indians of
Maine; in 1734 James Oglethorpe made a treaty at Char-
lottetown, in Georgia, with the Spanish governor of Florida;
and early in the 1750's Governor Dinwiddie corresponded
with the governor of Canada over the ownership of the Ohio
Valley and sent George Washington on a quasi-diplomatic

mission to the French military governor of Fort Le Boeuf in western Pennsylvania to request him to get out until the two sovereigns could decide to which that territory belonged. During that same decade, Governor Clinton of New York and Governor Shirley of Massachusetts carried on an active correspondence with the governor of French Canada relative to the extents and the boundaries of the English and French possessions in North America. (*See Reading No. 35.*) All through the colonial period, the governors of the colonies also negotiated with the chiefs of the Indian tribes along their frontiers as with foreign or semi-foreign potentates.

In all these dealings with non-English peoples, the Americans acquired experience in "international relations." More important still, they formulated, on the basis of what they considered their own "enlightened self-interest," a set of habits of mind, or policies, that should properly be seen as the earliest American diplomatic policies, which remained consistently the basic lines of expression of American international interest for centuries.

In the negotiations of the seaboard colonies with the Dutch of New Netherland and the French of Acadia, their principal interest was commerce. As their prosperity depended upon the export of their products, they were interested in the freedom to go and come in the ports of these non-English colonies. They therefore wrote this freedom into their treaties with the Dutch and French colonies. During the eighteenth century, as we have seen, the colonial merchants developed a prosperous trade with the non-English colonies in the West Indies. This trade was opposed by the planters of the British West Indies and by certain elements in England. But the Americans justified this economic side of their international relations by a set of ideas expressed, as already noted, by such leaders as Jeremiah Dummer of New England, James Logan of Philadelphia, and Cadwallader Colden of New York. On the whole, these ideas added up to a doctrine of freedom of international commerce for the colonies, even though it might ostensibly run contrary to the British navigation system and the international doctrines of mercantilism.

Despite their strong feeling of isolation from European squabbles, the Americans were never averse to conflict in

America when such conflicts were thought to be necessary
in the light of the Americans' "enlightened self-interest."
The colonies—most of them, at any rate—gladly participated in wars against the Indians whenever they expected
to acquire ownership of Indian lands thereby, even in
times of peace in Europe, and they participated in the
"intercolonial" wars for the sake of the booty or other
winnings they hoped to gain from them. Georgia, for example, gladly took up arms against Florida in 1740, and
most of the colonists in the continental colonies supported
with enthusiasm the imperialistic British expedition against
Cartagena in 1741.

Indeed, apart from commercial interest, it was probably
the westward expansion of the colonies across the continent
that produced the most vigorous expressions of American
thinking relative to international relations. And as it was
the French colonies that blocked this expansion, it was
against France and its colonies that most of this thinking
was directed.

By the middle of the eighteenth century, the "inevitable"
conflict between the French and British empires in North
America had reached a climax. American commentators
were both critical of British foreign policy (which, in their
view, had sacrificed the interests of the Empire to a weak
pacification in Europe in the Peace of Aix-la-Chapelle in
1748) and increasingly outspoken in their imperialistic in-
sistence that France be driven out of America. Thus, Dr.
William Douglass of Boston took the British ministry to
task for returning to France the fortress Louisbourg, on
Cape Breton Island, which had been taken by the New
Englanders in 1745. It was by this action, he said, that the
Americans had enabled Britain to come off victorious in the
war. But Douglass acknowledged France's ownership of the
interior of the continent and expressed a willingness to
accept a boundary line between the French and English
colonies that would lie just west of the Alleghenies.

As the "cold war" in North America waxed warmer
between 1750 and 1754, the thinking of many American
leaders moved steadily toward a more and more imperialistic position, toward the demand that the French be driven
out of the continent and that it be occupied entirely by the
British. This trend was represented by Thomas Hutchin-

son, a leading politician and judge in Boston, and by Rev. Charles Chauncy, also of Boston. But the clearest pronouncement of this logical conclusion of Angloamerican imperialism was made by another minister, the Rev. Jonathan Mayhew. Mayhew, in his election sermon to the Massachusetts legislature in 1754 (*see Reading No. 36*), declared that "there must, sooner or later, be some great turn of affairs upon this Continent, which will put it out of our power, or out of theirs [*the French*], to dispute about boundaries; . . . . The continent is not wide enough for us both; and they are resolved to have the whole." This religious recognition of the inevitability of a showdown with the French empire in America was supported by a passionate diatribe against French Catholicism and the absolutism of French government and by an exhortation to carry forward the struggle for the domination of the continent in order to preserve British "liberties." This was essentially a religion-inspired imperialism; the crusade Mayhew preached would be one to make North America safe for British "liberty." But Mayhew's thought was typical of much of American thinking with regard to the relations of the colonies with those of other nations, particularly France and Spain.

Running through the experiences of the colonial period, then, there may clearly be seen the growth, out of their experiences, of certain ideas: the doctrine of isolation from Europe, the doctrines of freedom of the seas, the concept of manifest destiny, and the use of the diplomatic machinery of government to promote territorial expansion. All these aspects of American thought had their origins in the colonial experience; all persisted until the end of the frontier and the advent of the Industrial Revolution changed the directions of American "enlightened self-interest"; some of them are still powerful influences in the determination of American foreign policy.

# THE ORIGINS OF AMERICAN NATIONAL SELF-CONSCIOUSNESS

In the colonial period of American history there was born among the Americans a body of ideas and sentiments about themselves that would eventually become an American national self-consciousness. Never, however, during the colonial period, did the Angloamericans think of themselves as constituting a separate nation. Their nation, to which they paid their highest loyalty, was the British Empire. Each citizen's "country," toward which he felt a certain local patriotism (as distinguished from nationalism), was his colony—Virginia, South Carolina, Massachusetts, and the rest. It was only very late in the colonial period that the term "America" came to represent a concept that was clear and meaningful, a concept to which a man might also pay a certain type of loyalty.

**The Self-consciousness of American Britons.** Colonial self-consciousness was of slow growth. Furthermore, it developed entirely within the larger concept of the British Empire as a whole. The inhabitants of the British colonies in America, during roughly the first half century of their history, were Englishmen born in England. The inhabitants of the southern colonies, especially, thought of themselves as English citizens and of their colonies simply as overseas extensions of the society of England itself. With the exception of the Puritan minority that founded New England, Englishmen had generally looked upon their migration to America as merely an expansion of English society. Walter

Raleigh's famous remark about Virginia, that "I shall yet live to see it an English nation," probably did not mean a new and separate English nation, but rather an extension of the old.

This basic feeling of Britishness, indeed, characterized the feelings and the loyalties of the Americans right down to the Revolution. They gloried in the name of Britons, and they took great pride in the things that characterized the British nation: their "liberty," their "rights of Englishmen," and their "constitution." A writer in the Boston *Independent Advertiser,* for example, wrote in 1749 that "Our Constitution is English, which is another name for free and happy: And it is without Doubt the perfectest model of Civil Government that has ever been in the World; . . . . Our Nation [*the British*] has always prided itself upon this its happy constitution, has shown the quickest Sense of Resentment at all attempts to violate it, and has ever judged the Calamities of a Civil War more tolerable than the Loss of it."

Even in their disputes with the government of the Empire, the Americans always considered themselves Englishmen, members of the "English" or "British" nation, with all the rights and privileges of Englishmen. Their protests against the Navigation Laws and Acts of Trade, for example, were based upon the outraged feeling that those laws discriminated against the American Englishmen by denying them rights that Englishmen in England enjoyed. At the same time, the Americans celebrated the glories of English achievements, such as victories in war, as their own. They shared in the catastrophic Cartegena expedition of 1741, for example, with great enthusiasm, suffused (apart from the desire for booty) with a feeling of British nationalistic ardor. In 1753 Benjamin Franklin still thought of the people of the colonies as so many "British subjects *on this side of the water* . . . [*who ought to be*] on the same footing with those of Great Britain" and the colonies as "so many counties gained to Great Britain." Again, in his famous pamphlet on Guadeloupe, written in the midst of the Seven Years War, Franklin said, "if ever there was a *national war,* this is truly such a one: a war in which the interest of the *whole* nation is directly and fundamentally concerned."

Poets, too, such as Nathaniel Ames and Frances Hopkinson, celebrated the joint ideals and nationalistic mythos of "British" military glory. (*See Chapter 7.*) The feeling of solidarity, the emotional sense of being at one with other Britons everywhere, was characteristic of American thinking throughout the colonies. And it remained so, until the very eve of the American Declaration of Independence.

**The Self-Consciousness of British Colonials.**   In contrast with the generally shared feeling of British nationalism, there had been growing among the Americans, almost from the very beginning of their history, a certain sense of differentness from the mother country and a feeling that the new colonial societies were in certain ways unique. This feeling was particularly strong and self-conscious among the Puritan leaders who founded New England. John Winthrop, for example, was convinced that God was especially interested in the Puritan project for a new society; Edward Johnson, in his *Wonder-Working Providence of Zion's Saviour,* interpreted the settlement of New England explicitly in these terms. Rev. Cotton Mather expressed the same idea in the prologue to his *Magnalia Christi Americana,* and said, in his *Theopolis Americana.* (*See Reading No. 37.*) "There are many Arguments to perswade us That our Glorious Lord, will have an Holy City in America; a City, the Street whereof shall be Pure Gold."

By Mather's time, however, something new had been added. For to Mather's Puritan self-consciousness had been added a sense of the differentness of America from England, quite apart from any religious consideration. And Mather's Americanism was closely related to that of Robert Beverley, whose *History of Virginia,* published at almost exactly the same time as Mather's *Magnalia,* was one of the first expressions of the nascent American self-consciousness in the southern colonies. This more secular sense of differentness, of uniqueness, of importance in the history of the world, achieved expression in the writings of a whole generation of history writers, as we have seen. All of these colonial historians wrote of their own provinces, each one seeking to portray the peculiar beginnings, achievements, and virtues of his own society.

This nascent provincial self-consciousness was becoming clear in the thought of some Americans about their governments. Thus, Jonathan Mayhew, echoing the satisfaction all British Americans felt in enjoying the liberties and rights of Britons, was convinced that the constitution of his own "country," Massachusetts, was by far the best of all those in the Empire, even that of England itself. As he said, "Our ancestors [*who settled Massachusetts*] . . . were a religious, brave and virtuous set of men, whose love of liberty, civil and religious, brought them from their native land, into the American deserts. By their generous care, it is, under the smiles of a gracious providence, that we have now here a goodly heritage; . . . Tho' we are not an independent state, yet, Heaven be thank'd! We are a free people."

Furthermore, this feeling of devotion to one's "country" could achieve the power of an intense emotional patriotism, as, for example, when Rev. Samuel Davies of Virginia urged the Virginia militia on to an inspired struggle against their French and Indian enemies. (*See Reading No. 38.*)

This feeling of devotion to one's own colonial society may be described as a local or provincial patriotism—the love of the land where one lives. It in no way conflicted with the generally shared feeling of British nationalism, which was a loyalty to a larger, quasi-mystical entity known as the British nation, made up of all Englishmen everywhere. In the feelings of the Americans, one's colonial society was but a variant of the national, or "imperial," British society. One's loyalty was of a dual sort: the two loyalties coincided.

**The Self-Consciousness of Americans.** Meanwhile, a concept of "America"—all the colonies taken together—was growing among the colonists, especially those on the continent of North America. And along with the concept, there was growing a sense of the peculiar and glorious future of this segment of the Empire. This feeling for "America," which was to flower on the eve of the Revolution, expressed itself about the middle of the century, in William Douglass' *Summary . . . of the British Settlements in North America.* Douglass' book was largely inspired by his hatred of the French, a sentiment that also inspired William Livingston's *Review of Military Operations in North America* (1757) and Archibald Kennedy's *The Importance of Gaining the Friendship of the Indians*

(1751), to which was appended Benjamin Franklin's proposal for a voluntary union of the colonies, which became one of the bases of the Plan of Union adopted by the Albany Congress of 1754.

This growing sense of America as a whole was much more than a rationalization of the necessity for a united defense, or common front, in the face of a common enemy. It was a genuine, enthusiastic anticipation of the peculiar and glorious future of America—a sense of the "manifest destiny" of this new segment of the British Empire. Somewhat in the mood of Cotton Mather, this sense of destiny found religious expression in Jonathan Edwards' *History of Redemption,* whose author was convinced that the millennium of God, the ultimate climax of all history, would be realized in America. In more secular vein, Nathaniel Ames, in his *Astronomical Diary* for 1758, saluted in glowing terms (*see Reading No. 39*) those Americans who would be enjoying the glories of America a century after his time.

Nor was this "American" self-consciousness only political; it was also manifesting itself in the thinking of Americans with regard to their cultural development. By about the middle of the eighteenth century, many Americans were recognizing that the colonies were developing a culture that was peculiarly their own. There was even a demand among some intellectual leaders for the conscious and deliberate creation of an "American" culture. Thus, the *American Magazine* published in Philadelphia in 1757 and 1758, proposed, among other things, to serve as a vehicle of American information and cultural creativity to England—a sort of American "Review" that would constitute a continuing American contribution to British literature, policy, and culture. The editor complained that the people of the mother-country paid far too little attention to the colonies; the *American Magazine* would inform them. As for American cultural development, "We shall always make it one principal end of this work, to encourage rising genius in this young country, and nurse up a set of able and honest writers, in the various branches of polite letters, for the benefit of the present times, and of posterity. . . ."

There was still no conflict between this mounting sense of the differentness of "America" and of loyalty to it, on the one side, and the Angloamericans' loyalty to the British nation—they called it "Empire"—of which the colonies were parts, on the other. In the course of their experiences in America, nevertheless, the Americans had developed new loyalties, to their separate colonies and to America as a whole. These loyalties were peculiar to Americans. They did not exist in England. And Philip Freneau and Hugh Henry Brackenridge, in their "Poem on the Rising Glory of America" (*see Reading No. 40*), written for the Princeton commencement of 1771, could sing of "America,"

> Hail happy land
> The Seat of empire the abode of kings,
> The final stage where time shall introduce
> Renowned characters, and glorious works
> Of high invention and of wond'rous art,
> While not the ravages of time shall waste
> 'Till he himself has run his long career;
> 'Till all those glorious orbs of light on high
> The rolling wonders that surround the ball,
> Drop from their spheres extinguish'd and consum'd,
> When final ruin with her fiery car
> Rides o'er creation, and all natures works
> Are lost in chaos and the womb of night,

without the slightest diminution of their loyalty to "the Empire."

The supreme loyalty of the Americans, of course, was their loyalty to the British Empire-nation, whose symbol was its king, and this loyalty they shared with their fellow Englishmen in England. But their characteristically American loyalties, both to their "countries" and to "America," were new psychological phenomena peculiar to themselves. These psychological forces, if not accommodated by Britain to the facts of history, would dissolve the Empire and become the psychological bases for new states and a new nation.

# Part II
# READINGS

## BENJAMIN FRANKLIN ON THE RELATIONSHIP OF AMERICANS TO THE BRITISH EMPIRE (1756)*

*Benjamin Franklin believed, in 1756, that the British subjects in the colonies had all the rights of other Englishmen, including that of representation in Parliament. The colonies were integral parts of the British Empire; any laws that discriminated against them should be repealed. Franklin proposed, in effect, a single Parliament for the whole British empire, one of the first such proposals ever made. Such a Parliament, however, would in no way have replaced the separate colonial legislatures. Thus, his scheme curiously anticipates the later organization of the United States. Franklin soon recognized the impracticality of the idea of American representation in Parliament and gave it up. Its significance lies in the concept of a politically unified empire, with exactly equal rights and privileges of all the British subjects in it, everywhere.*

✓         ✓         ✓

Since the conversation your Excellency was pleased to honour me with, on the subject of uniting the colonies more intimately with Great Britain, by allowing them representatives in parliament, I have something further considered that matter, and am of opinion, that such a union would be very acceptable to the colonies, provided they had a reasonable number of representatives allowed them; and that all the old acts of Parliament restraining the trade or cramping the manufactures of the colonies be at the same time repealed, and the British subjects on this side the water put, in those respects, on the same footing with those in Great Britain, till the new Parliament, represent-

* Benjamin Franklin to William Shirley, Dec. 22, 1754. *The Papers of Benjamin Franklin,* ed. Leonard W. Labaree (5 vols. to date. New Haven: Yale University Press, 1959- ), Vol. V, pp. 449-451. Reprinted by permission of Yale University Press.

ing the whole, shall think it for the interest of the whole to
reënact some or all of them. It is not that I imagine so many
representatives will be allowed the colonies, as to give any
great weight by their numbers; but I think there might be sufficient to occasion those laws to be better and more impartially
considered, and perhaps to overcome the interest of a petty
corporation, or of any particular set of artificers or traders of
England, who heretofore seem, in some instances, to have
been more regarded than all the colonies, or than was con-
sistent with the general interest, or best national good. . . .

I should hope too, that by such a union, the people of Great
Britain, and the people of the colonies, would learn to consider
themselves, as not belonging to a different community with different interests, but to one community with one interest; which
I imagine would contribute to strengthen the whole, and greatly
lessen the danger of future separation.

It is, I suppose, agreed to be the general interest of any state,
that its people be numerous and rich; . . . . The iron manu-
facture employs and enriches British subjects, but is it of any
importance to the state, whether the manufacturers live at
Birmingham, or Sheffield, or both, since they are still within
its bounds, and their wealth and persons still at its command? . . .

Now I look upon the colonies as so many counties gained
to Great Britain, and more advantageous to it than if they
had been gained out of the seas around its coasts, and joined
to its land: For being in different climates, they afford greater
variety of produce, and being separated by the ocean, they
increase much more its shipping and seamen; and since they
are all included in the British empire, which has only extended
itself by their means; and the strength and wealth of the parts
are the strength and wealth of the whole; what imports it to
the general state, whether a merchant, a smith, or a hatter grow
rich in Old or New England? And if, through increase of
people, two smiths are wanted for one employed before, why
may not the new smith be allowed to live and thrive in the
new country, as well as the old one in the old? In fine, why
should the countenance of a state be partially afforded to its
people, unless it be most in favour of those who have most
merit? And if there be any difference, those who have most
contributed to enlarge Britain's empire and commerce, increase
her strength, her wealth, and the numbers of her people, at
the risk of their own lives and private fortunes in new and
strange countries, methinks ought rather to expect some preference.

# — Reading No. 2 —

## REV. JOHN BARNARD ON THE RIGHT OF REVOLUTION (1746)*

*Many of the early American political thinkers, who based their thinking upon the theory of natural rights and the social compact, found it only logical that the people, who created government in the first place, could remove a tyrannical government whenever they thought it desirable, by force if necessary. Rev. John Barnard, of New England, was one of the many preachers who expounded this theory.*

✓          ✓          ✓

For one person alone to have the Government of a People in his hands, would be too great a Temptation. It tends to excite and draw forth the Pride of man, to make him unsufferably haughty; it gives him too much liberty to exert [?] his Corruptions; and it encourages him to become a Tyrant and an oppressor, to dispense with Laws and break the most solemn oaths. To proceed so far in his unrighteous Practices, that his Subjects weary of the doctrine of passive obedience and non-resistance, are necessitated to plead their own cause and vindicate Their Rights by Measures which for a long time they were loth to make use of . . . [*as in the time of King James II the English people*] armed themselves in defence of their Religion and Liberties; the Consequence of which was his abdicating the Throne.

* John Barnard, *The Presence of the Great God in the Assembly of Political Rulers* (Boston, 1746), pp. 11-12.

# — Reading No. 3 —

## CADWALLADER COLDEN: THE TORY IDEA OF THE BALANCE OF POWERS*

*Cadwallader Colden, who eventually became Lieutenant-Governor of the Colony of New York, followed the English constitutional theorists who felt that the three elements in government were the "Monarchical, the aristocraticall, and the Democratical," as represented in the English constitution by the king, the House of Lords, and the House of Commons. His objective, as he applied this theory to the province of New York, was to check the growing power of the New York Assembly.*

✓         ✓         ✓

It is the great Happiness of the People of the Province of New York that the Government is form'd as near as may be upon the same Plan with that of our Mother Country. . . .

This Constitution consists in a proper Ballance between the Monarchical Aristocraticall & Democratical forms of Government of which our Constitution is compounded & whenever the Ballance is alter'd by an overbearing power in any of these three parts of our Constitution the Constitution it self is so far alter'd & such alteration has been allwise accompanied with many Disturbances & often with Civil Wars & Revolutions of the State. . . .

From what appears from our own History & I believe from the History of all Nations a mixed Govern't runs more risk from to Great a Power in the Monarchical part or Democratical than from the Aristocratical & indeed more danger from an over power in the Democratical than from that of the Monarchical because People are allwise jealous of the Monarchy but fond of every thing that encreases the Democracy.

* Cadwallader Colden, *The Letters and Papers of Cadwallader Colden*, vol. IX (*Collections of the New York Historical Society, LXVIII*), pp. 251-257.

## ECONOMIC INDIVIDUALISM: THE
## SAYINGS OF "POOR RICHARD"*

*The almost universal American ideas of individual thrift, industry, and material self-improvement were nowhere expressed more pithily than in the "wise sayings" that appeared annually in* Poor Richard, *Benjamin Franklin's famous almanac. A compendium of these sayings, often referred to as "Father Abraham's Speech," appeared in* Poor Richard Improved *for the year 1758.*

I stopt my Horse lately where a great Number of People were collected at a Vendue [*public auction*] of Merchant Goods. The Hour of Sale not being come, they were conversing on the Badness of the Times, and one of the Company call'd to a plain clean old Man, with white Locks, Pray, Father Abraham, what think you of the Times? Won't these heavy Taxes quite ruin the Country? What would you advise us to? . . . Father Abraham stood up, and reply'd, if you'd have my Advice, I'll give it you in short, for a Word to the Wise is enough, and many Words won't fill a Bushel, as Poor Richard says. . . .

However let us hearken to good Advice, and something may be done for us; God helps them that help themselves, as Poor Richard says in his Almanack of 1733. . . . Sloth, like Rust, consumes faster than Labour wears, while the used key is always bright, as Poor Richard says. But dost Thou love Life, then do not squander Time, for that's The Stuff Life is made of, as Poor Richard says. . . . The sleeping Fox catches no Poultry, and . . . There will be sleeping enough in the grave . . . Lost Time is never found again. . . . Let us then be up and doing, and doing to the Purpose; so by Diligence shall we do more with less Perplexity. Sloth makes all Things difficult, but Industry all easy, as Poor Richard says; and He

* *Poor Richard Improved: Being an Almanack and Ephemeris . . . for the Year of our Lord 1758* (Philadelphia, 1757).

that riseth late, must trot all Day, and shall scarce overtake his Business at Night. . . . [So] Drive thy Business, let not that drive Thee; and Early to Bed, and early to rise, makes a Man healthy, wealthy and wise.

So what signifies wishing and hoping for better Times. We may make these Times better if we bestir ourselves. . . . He that lives upon Hope will die fasting. . . . He that hath a Trade hath an Estate, and He that hath a Calling hath an office of Profit and Honour . . . for, as Poor Richard says, at the working Man's House Hunger looks in, but dares not enter. . . . Then plough deep, while Sluggards sleep and you shall have Corn to sell and to keep, says Poor Dick. . . .

So much for Industry, my Friends, and attention to one's own Business; but to these we must add Frugality, if we would make our Industry more certainly successful. . . . A fat Kitchen makes a lean Will, as Poor Richard says; and

Many Estates are spent in the Getting,
Since Women for Tea forsook Spinning and Knitting,
And Men for Punch forsook Hewing and Splitting. . . .

But what Madness must it be to run in debt for these Superfluities! . . . for, as Poor Richard says, The second Vice is Lying, the first is running in Debt. . . . But Poverty often deprives a Man of all Spirit and Virtue: Tis hard for an empty Bag to stand upright, as Poor Richard truly says. . . . So rather go to Bed supperless than rise in Debt.

Get what you can, and what you get hold;
Tis the Stone that will turn all your Lead into Gold. . . .

# — Reading No. 5 —

## "PHILALETHES" (REV. ELISHA WILLIAMS) ON THE INDIVIDUAL'S NATURAL RIGHT TO THE OWNERSHIP OF PROPERTY*

*The economic individualism of the Commercial Revolution had come to America with the first colonists. This mood was reinforced by the experience of the settlers as they achieved economic success and stability in the conquest of the wilderness, and it found a perfect rationalization in the doctrine that what a man produces is his own by natural right and cannot be taken away from him except by his consent. Rev. Elisha Williams was one of many American thinkers who explained and supported this economic doctrine in terms of the American experiment.*

✓          ✓          ✓

Reason teaches us that all Men are naturally equal in Respect of Jurisdiction or Dominion one over another. . . . And as Reason tells us, all are born thus naturally equal, i.e. with an equal Right to their Persons; so also with an equal Right to their Preservation; and therefore to such Things as Nature affords for their Subsistence. . . . And every Man having a Property in his own Person, The Labour of his Body and the Work of his Hands are properly his own, to which no one has a Right but himself; it will therefore follow that when he removes any Thing out of the State that Nature has provided and left it in, he has mixed his Labour with it and joined something to it that is his own, and thereby makes it his Property. . . . Thus every Man having a natural Right to (or

---

* "Philalethes" [Elisha Williams], *The Essential Rights and Liberties of Protestants. A Seasonable Plea for The Liberty of Conscience, and The Right of Private Judgment, In Matters of Religion, Without any Controul from human Authority* (Boston, 1744), pp. 2-3.

being the Proprietor of) his own Person and his own Actions and Labour and to what he can honestly acquire by his Labour, which we call Property; it certainly follows, that no Man can have a Right to the 'Person or 'Property of another: And if every Man has a Right to his 'Person and 'Property; he has also a Right to defend them, and a Right to all the necessary Means of Defence, and so has a Right of punishing all Insults upon this Person and Property. . . .

## — Reading No. 6 —

# BENJAMIN FRANKLIN ON THE LABOR THEORY OF VALUE*

*In his discussion of the problem of a circulating medium, or money, Benjamin Franklin got into a discussion of the nature of value itself. Borrowing many of his ideas from the English economist, Sir William Petty, Franklin concluded that the value of a commodity, with certain special exceptions, is determined by the amount of labor required to produce it.*

✓          ✓          ✓

For many Ages, those Parts of the World which are engaged in Commerce, have fixed upon Gold and Silver as the chief and most proper Materials for this Medium; they being in themselves valuable Metals for their Fineness, Beauty, and Scarcity. By these, particularly by Silver, it has been usual to value all Things else: But as Silver itself is of no certain permanent Value, being worth more or less according to its Scarcity or Plenty, therefore it seems requisite to fix upon Something else, more proper to be made a *Measure of Values*, and this I take to be *Labour*.

By Labour may the Value of Silver be measured as well as other Things. As, Suppose one Man employed to raise Corn, while another is digging and refining Silver; at the Year's End, or at any other Period of Time, the compleat Produce of Corn, and that of Silver, are the natural Price of each other; and if one be twenty Bushels, and the other twenty Ounces, then an Ounce of that Silver is worth the Labour of raising a Bushel of that Corn. Now if by the Discovery of some nearer, more easy or plentiful Mines, a Man may get Forty Ounces of Silver as easily as formerly he did Twenty, and the same Labour is

---

* Benjamin Franklin, *A Modest Inquiry into the Nature and Necessity of a Paper Currency*. Reprinted in *The Papers of Benjamin Franklin*, ed. Leonard W. Labaree, Vol. I, pp. 149-153. Reproduced by permission of Yale University Press.

still required to raise Twenty Bushels of Corn, then Two
Ounces of Silver will be worth no more than the same Labour
of raising one Bushel of Corn, and that Bushel of Corn will
be as cheap at two Ounces, as it was before at one; *caeteris
paribus.*

Thus the Riches of a Country are to be valued by the
Quantity of Labour its Inhabitants are able to purchase, and
not by the Quantity of Silver and Gold they possess; which will
purchase more or less Labour, and therefore is more or less
valuable, as is said before, according to its Scarcity or Plenty.
As those Metals have grown much more plentiful in Europe
since the Discovery of America, so they have sunk in Value
exceedingly; for, to instance in England, formerly one Penny
of Silver was worth a Days Labour, but now it is hardly worth
the sixth Part of a Days Labour; because not less than Six-
pence will purchase the Labour of a Man for a Day in any
Part of that Kingdom; which is wholly to be attributed to the
much greater Plenty of Money now in England than formerly.
And yet perhaps England is in effect no richer now than at
that Time; because as much Labour might be purchas'd, or
Work got done of almost any kind, for £100 then, as will now
require or is now worth £600. . . .

Trade in general being nothing else but the exchange of
Labour for Labour, the Value of all Things is, as I have said
before, most justly measured by Labour. Now suppose I put
my Money into a Bank, and take out a Bill for the Value; if
this Bill at the Time of my receiving it, would purchase me
the Labour of one hundred Men for twenty Days; but some
time after will only purchase the Labour of the same Number
of Men for fifteen Days; it is plain the Bill has sunk in Value
one fourth Part. Now Silver and Gold being of no permanent
Value; and as this Bill is founded on Money, and therefore
to be esteemed as such, it may be that the Occasion of this
Fall is the increasing Plenty of Gold and Silver, by which
Money is one fourth Part less valuable than before, and therefore one fourth more is given of it for the same Quantity of
Labour; and if Land is not become more plentiful by some
proportionate Decrease of the People, one fourth Part more of
Money is given for the same quantity of Land, whereby it
appears that it would have been more profitable to me to have
laid that Money out in Land which I put into the Bank, than
to place it there and take a Bill for it. And it is certain that
the Value of Money has been continually sinking in England
for several Ages past, because it has been continually increasing in Quantity. But if Bills could be taken out of a Bank in
Europe on a Land Security, it is probable the Value of such
Bills would be more certain and steady, because the Number

of Inhabitants continue to be near the same in those Countries
from Age to Age. . . .

Yet farther, in order to make a true Estimate of the Value
of Money, we must distinguish between Money as it is Bullion,
which is Merchandize, and as by being coin'd it is made a Currency: For its Value as a Merchandize, and its Value as a
Currency, are two distinct Things; and each may possibly rise
and fall in some Degree independent of the other. Thus if the
Quantity of Bullion increases in a Country, it will proportion-
ably decrease in Value; but if at the same Time the Quantity
of current Coin should decrease, (supposing Payments may not
be made in Bullion) what Coin there is will rise in Value as
a Currency, i.e. People will give more Labour in Manufactures
for a certain Sum of ready Money.

In the same Manner must we consider a *Paper Currency*
founded on Land; as it is Land, and as it is a Currency:

*Money as Bullion, or as Land, is valuable by so much Labour
as it costs to procure that Bullion or Land.*

*Money, as a Currency, has an Additional Value by so much
Time and Labour as it saves in the Exchange of Commodities.*

If, as a Currency, it saves one Fourth Part of the Time and
Labour of a Country; it has, on that Account, one Fourth
added to its original Value. . . .

From these Considerations it may be gathered, that in all
the Degrees between having no Money in a Country, and
Money sufficient for the Trade, it will rise and fall in Value
as a Currency, in Proportion to the Decrease or Increase of
its Quantity: And if their may be at some Time more than
enough, the Overplus will have no Effect towards making the
Currency, as a Currency, of less Value than when there was
but enough; because such Overplus will not be used in Trade,
but be some other way disposed of.

## JEREMIAH DUMMER ON THE ECONOMIC AUTONOMY OF THE AMERICAN COLONIES IN THE BRITISH EMPIRE*

*In the first quarter of the eighteenth century, there was a strong move in England to bring the American colonies more closely under the economic and political control of the central imperial government in England. This would involve the revocation of some or all of the colonial charters that permitted the colonies so much self-direction; it was also expected to involve a further limitation upon the free growth of the colonial economies. Jeremiah Dummer, agent in England for the colony of Connecticut, wrote a famous pamphlet defending the original charters and presenting a convincing economic argument to show that the prosperity of the colonies, achieved in relative freedom from economic restraint, really was the base of the economic prosperity of England itself.*

✓     ✓     ✓

Why then should not Great-Britain form the same Judgment, and proceed by the like Measures in regard to her American Dominions, from whence she receives the greatest Advantages? It were no difficult Task to prove that London has risen out of the Plantations, and not out of England. Tis to them we [*England*] owe our vast Fleets of Merchant Ships, and consequently the Increase of our Seamen, and Improvement of our Navigation. 'Tis their Tobacco, Sugar, Fish, Oil, Logwood and other Commodities, which have enabled us to support our [*English*] Trade in Europe, to bring the Ballance of some Countries in our Favour, which would otherwise be against us, and to make the Figure we do at present, and have done for near a Century past, in all Parts of the Commercial World.

The Mother Kingdom must therefore needs rejoice in the

* Jeremiah Dummer, *A Defense of the New-England Charters* (London, 1721), pp. 38-40.

Prosperity of every one of her Colonies, because it is her own Prosperity. . . .

The only Interest of the People [*of the colonies*] is to thrive and flourish in their Trade, which is the true Interest of the Crown and Nation, because they reap the Profit of it. . . . The Trade of a young Plantation is like a tender Plant, & should be cherish'd with the fondest Care; but if instead of that, it meets with the rough Hand of Oppression, it will soon die. The proper Nursery for this Plant is a free Government, where the Laws are Sacred, Property secure, & Justice not only impartially but expeditiously distributed. . . .

As this is evident, so is it that whatever injuries the Trade of the Plantations, must in Proportion affect Great-Britain, the Source and Center of their Commerce; from whence they have their Manufactures, whither they make their Returns, and where all their Superlucration is lodg'd. The Blow then may strike the Colonies first, but it comes Home at last, and falls heaviest on our selves.

# CADWALLADER COLDEN ON THE FREEDOM OF INTERNATIONAL COMMERCE*

*During the eighteenth century the northern colonies developed a profitable trade in foodstuffs, fish, sugar, molasses, and other commodities with the foreign colonies in the Caribbean area, and especially with the French islands of Guadeloupe and Martinique. This commerce, which in itself was entirely legal (so long as it did not violate the Navigation Acts, which it often did), was greatly resented by the British West Indies colonies and was a constant source of irritation to the imperial administration in London. It became particularly irritating, of course, in time of war, when it became, in effect, "trading with the enemy." Before and during the Seven Years War, orders were sent to the colonial governors to stop it. But even the most loyal governors saw that a stoppage of this trade would be a blow at the economic prosperity of the colonies. Cadwallader Colden, Lieutenant-Governor of New York, queried the wisdom of the suppression of this trade with an economic argument that was in essence an argument for freedom of commerce.*

      ✓            ✓           ✓

I have the honour of your commands of the 23ᵈ of August in relation to an illegal and pernicious trade, carried on by the King's subjects in North America, to French islands and French settlements on the Continent. . . . [*It is true that*] the merchants of this place [*New York*] have been too generally concerned in this trade, and that the merchants of Philadelphia have been more so. . . .

Now Sir, after I have given you what information I have obtain'd, permit me to tell you, what has been said in excuse;

---

* Cadwallader Colden to William Pitt, October 27 and December 27, 1760. New York Public Library, Manuscripts Division, "Colden Papers."

it is avered, that this trade has been highly advantageous to
Great Britain, by the great Quantities of British Manufactures
[*disposed of*], in value far exceeding the values of the provisions, and by the large returns in sugars; and some pretend
they can demonstrate this against the force of all contradic-
tion. . . .

𝄤      𝄤      𝄤

On the 6th instant I received a letter from General Amherst,
inclosing two letters to him. . . . These letters contain'd general information of illicit trade carried on in this place. I laid
them before the Council. . . .

I observed that the gentlemen of the Council distinguished
between trade with the Ennemie's Colonies and trade with
neutral ports. All trade with the enemy was allowed to be
prohibited; but that the trade with the neutral ports in the
West Indies is only illegal, under certain circumstances and in
certain commodities, and that this trade came not under the
view of his Majesties orders of the 23$^d$ of August last signified
by your letter of that date.

Tho' as to my own part . . . I shall do my utmost to dis-
courage all illegal trade . . . ; yet I think it may be of some
use to inform you of some remarks made while these inquiries
were before the Council.

1st The prohibition of exporting provisions from any of the
Colonies extends in general to every place except his Majesties'
dominions. Yet, as the plain view of the Act is only to prevent
the Ennemies being supplied with provisions, it cannot be intended to prevent sending of provisions to the Portiguees [*sic*]
and Spanish islands, from whence all the wines consumed in
America are imported; because all the provisions imported to
these islands are consumed in them and never reexported; and
if no provisions be allowed to be sent thither for the purchase
of wines, they must be paid in cash by Bills of Exchanges with
evident prejudice to the trade of Great Britain. . . .

2nd It was affirmed, that while the exportation of provisions
to neutral ports from the Colonies is absolutely prohibited,
great quantities of provisions are openly and with proper clearances carried to the neutral port[*s*] from Great Britain and
Ireland, from whence it was infer'd that the prohibition to the
Colonies cannot serve the purposes of the Act, but it's evidently
of prejudice to the trade of the Colonies, and in its consequence of prejudice to Great Britain; for without freedom in
trade the Colonies are not able to pay for the British manufactures consumed in them.

3$^d$ As to the foreign sugars it was observed that the sugars are generally imported in small vessels which tho most proper for that trade in the West Indies are not proper to carry them to Europe. . . .

4th The Spanish government has opened the Port of Monto Christi [*sic*] to the English, probably in order to strengthen that place as a barrier against the incroachments of the French. It is said the English are allowed to enter that Port freely, and that they on exportation receive the governors clearances for their cargo. At the same time it is said the French are debard [*sic*] from trade in that port, nevertheless it seems clear to me that the Spaniards are allowed to purchase sugars in the neighbouring French ports, and are allowed to sell them to the English at Monto Christi. The principal trades from these colonies is to this Port and other Spanish ports on Hispaniola where it is said the Spaniards on Cuba are likewish furnished. The vast increase lately in the exportation of British manufactures, to the Northern Colonies, more than can be occasioned by the British troops here, it is avered, is occasioned by this trade, and will appear by the Customs House books at London, Bristol & Liverpool. . . .

It seems evident to me that could a mutual intercourse in trade be obtain'd between the British & Spanish colonies, it must be highly advantageous to Great Britain. Or could a Treaty be made with the King of Spain by which the inhabitants of the Spanish Colonies were permitted to purchase provisions in the Northern colonies, and the inhabitants of the British colonies to sell provisions in the Spanish Colonies, and though this mutual intercourse were strictly confined to provisions only, it would greatly advance the trade and riches of Great Britain and cannot in any case be detrimental to it. In truth it appears evident to me that tho' Spain should not allow any trade to their colonies it must be of great advantage to Great Britain to allow the Spaniards a trade with their [*its*] colonies, because they can import nothing prejudicial to the trade of Great Britain.

The Northern Colonies cannot pay for their consumption of the British manufactures by their own produce, exported only to the British Colonies. . . . The result of the whole trade of North America, taking it in every shape, as [*is*] barely sufficient to pay the ballance due to Great Britain. The consumption of British manufactures in the Northern colonies increases in proportion to their ability to purchase them, and nothing can make the Northern colonies interfere with the British manufactures, but their poverty or inability to purchase. . . .

I have informed you Sir of these things, in hopes that my doing of it may be of use, not as an excuse for any remissness on my part. However as to presemtious or penal laws, I must beg leave to observe, that it is difficult to prosecute with success against the bent of the people, while they are under the prejudice to think that the Sugar Islands have gained a preference inconsistent with the true interest of their Mother Country, and whence prosecution fails of success it is of prejudice to the service it was designed to promote.

## — Reading No. 9 —

# AMERICA AS A MELTING-POT AND AS A REFUGE*

*Hector St. John de Crevecoeur was an astute Frenchman who lived in Angloamerica for a number of years. He was deeply impressed by American society as a refuge for poor Europeans who found it possible to find here a release from poverty and a refuge from other troubles in Europe, as well as by the more positive aspects of life in America represented by economic opportunity and by the social fluidity he saw here. He romanticized the phenomena he described; nevertheless, they were true.*

✗          ✗          ✗

In this great American asylum, the poor of Europe have by some means met together, and in consequence of various causes; to what purpose should they ask one another what countrymen they are? . . .

What attachment can a poor European have for a country where he had nothing? The knowledge of the language, the love of a few kindred as poor as himself, were the only cords that tied him: his country is now that which gives him land, bread, protection, and consequence: *Ubi panis ibi patria* [*where one earns his bread, there is his country*] is the motto of all emigrants. What then is the American, this new man? He is either an European, or the descendent of an European, hence that strange mixture of blood, which you will find in no other country. I could point out to you a family whose grandfather was an Englishman, whose wife was Dutch, whose son married a French woman, and whose present four sons have now four wives of different nations. *He* is an American, who leaving behind him all his ancient prejudices and manners, receives new ones from the new mode of life he has embraced, the new government he obeys, and the new rank he holds. He becomes an American by being received in the broad lap of our great

* Hector St. John Crevecoeur, *Letters from an American Farmer* (London, 1782), pp. 45-53.

*Alma Mater.* Here individuals of all nations are melted into a new race of men, whose labours and posterity will one day cause great changes in the world. Americans are the western pilgrims, who are carrying along with them that great mass of arts, sciences, vigour, and industry which began long since in the east; they will finish the great circle. The Americans were once scattered all over Europe; here they are incorporated into one of the finest systems of population which has ever appeared, and which will hereafter become distinct by the power of the different climates they inhabit. . . . The American is a new man, who acts upon new principles; he must therefore entertain new ideas, and form new opinions. From involuntary idleness, servile dependence, penury, and useless labour, he has passed to toils of a very different nature, rewarded by ample subsistence,—This is an American.

## HUGH JONES ON THE BENEFITS OF SLAVERY TO THE NEGRO (1724)*

*Hugh Jones was a resident of Virginia who in 1724 published a description of that colony for the benefit of Englishmen. He described slavery, which was so important to Virginia's economy, as one of the colony's universally established institutions, without the slightest feeling of criticism. In fact, he seemed to take a certain satisfaction in its benefits, even to the Negroes themselves.*

✦       ✦       ✦

The Negroes [*in Virginia*] are very numerous, some Gentlemen having Hundreds of them of all Sorts, to whom they bring great profit; for the Sake of which they are obliged to keep them well, and not over-work, starve, or famish them, besides other Inducements to favor them; which is done in a great Degree, to such especially that are laborious, careful, and honest; tho' indeed some Masters, careless of their own Interest or Reputation, are too cruel and negligent. . . .

Their Work (or Chimerical hard Slavery) is not very laborious; their greatest Hardship consisting in that they and their Posterity are not at their own Liberty or Disposal, but are the Property of their Owners; and when they are free, they know not how to provide so well for themselves generally; neither did they live so plentifully nor (many of them) so easily in their own Country, where they are made Slaves to one another, or taken captive by their Enemies. . . .

Several of them are taught to be Sawyers, Carpenters, Smiths, Coopers, &c, and though for the most Part they be none of the aptest or nicest, yet they are by Nature cut out for hard Labour and Fatigue, and will perform tolerably well; though they fall much short of an Indian, that has learn'd and seen

* Hugh Jones, *The Present State of Virginia* . . . (London 1724), pp. 37-38.

the same Things; and those Negroes make the best Servants, that have been Slaves in their own Country; for they that have been Kings and great Men there are generally lazy, haughty, and obstinate; whereas the others are sharper, better humoured, and more laborious. . . .

# SAMUEL SEWALL ON THE UNNATURAL CHARACTER OF SLAVERY (1700)*

*Samuel Sewall was a stern but kindly judge in Puritan Boston at the time of the turn of the seventeenth century into the eighteenth. He found slavery repugnant on humanitarian and religious grounds as well as on the grounds of expediency. His "Memorial," entitled "The Selling of Joseph," was one of the earliest anti-slavery tracts written in colonial America.*

✓          ✓          ✓

Forasmuch as Liberty is in real value next unto Life: None ought to part with it themselves, or deprive others of it, but upon most mature consideration. . . .

It is most certain that all Men, as they are the Sons of Adam, are Coheirs; and have equal Right unto Liberty, and all other outward Comforts of Life. . . . So that Originally, and Naturally, there is no such Thing as Slavery. Joseph was rightfully no more a Slave to his Brethren than they were to him; and they had no more Authority to Sell him, than they had to Slay him. . . . There is no proportion between Twenty Pieces of Silver, and Liberty. . . .

And all things considered, it would conduce more to the Welfare of the Province [*Massachusetts*], to have White Servants for a Term of Years, than to have Slaves for Life. Few can endure to hear of a Negro's being made free; and indeed they can seldom use their freedom well; yet their continual aspiring after their forbidden Liberty, renders them Unwilling Servants. And there is such a disparity in their Conditions, Colour & Hair, that they can never embody [*be assimilated*] with us, and grow up into orderly Families, to the peopling of the Land: but still remain in our Body Politic as a kind of exctavasat Blood [*i.e., blood outside the veins*]. As many Negro men as there are among us, so many empty places there are in our Train Bands, and the places taken up of Men tha┐

* Samuel Sewall, *The Selling of Joseph: A Memorial* (Boston┐ 1700).

might make Husbands for our Daughters. And the Sons and Daughters, of New England would become more like Jacob, and Rachel, if this Slavery were thrust quite out of doors. . . . It is likewise most lamentable to think, how in taking Negros out of Africa, and Selling of them here, That which God has joyned together men do boldly rend asunder; Men from their Country, Husbands from their Wives, Parents from their Children: How horrible is the Uncleanness, Mortality, if not Murder, that the Ships be guilty of that bring great Crouds of these miserable Men, and Women. Methinks, when we are bemoaning the barbarous Usage of our Friends and Kinsfolk in Africa, it might not be unseasonable to enquire whether we are not culpable in forcing the Africans to become Slaves amongst our selves. . . .

## — Reading No. 12 —

## THE ARGUMENT FOR ENCOURAGING IMMIGRATION (1749)*

*Most of the colonies favored the immigration of foreigners, on the ground that they supplied a much-needed labor force. There were some individuals who opposed the importation of Negroes on racial grounds; a few in Pennsylvania, notably Provost William Smith and Benjamin Franklin, expressed grave doubts about the wisdom of importing even the Germans, with their "boorish" non-English language and customs. The following selection is from an economic essay by an anonymous author published in* The Independent Advertiser *(Boston) in 1749.*

ꭥ       ꭥ       ꭥ

It must be a great Advantage to this Country [*Massachusetts*] to encourage as much as possible, Foreigners to settle amongst us; by this Means Labour would be cheap, and we might consequently with Ease increase our Manufactures, and supply our Wants out of our own Produce as well as export much more to foreign Countries: I cannot but look upon this as an Article of great importance, and very worthy the Attention of our Legislature: As the Law now stands, I fear the importation of Foreigners is rather discouraged than promoted. And if it would be as I think, no man can doubt an inestimable Advantage, to have our meanest Lands peopled; and if those which are already possessed need more Hands to produce what they are capable of producing, No Method should be left untried to procure an Advantage so needful, and so salutory to the Province; nor any Time lost in removing Impediments to so beneficial an Event: And it is well worth the Attention of our Superiors, whether it is not detrimental to the Community to allow such large Tracts of Land as have formerly been allowed to those who for a Course of Years have taken no Pains suitably to improve the

* *The Independent Advertiser* (Boston), Feb. 27, 1749.

same; also whether the Tenure and Condition of past Grants have been punctually complied with by Proprietors of Lands, and to oblige them either to settle their Lands, or quit them to those that will. . . .

# — Reading No. 13 —

# BENJAMIN FRANKLIN ON THE RAPID INCREASE OF THE AMERICAN POPULATION (1751)*

*The extremely rapid increase in the population of the Anglo-american colonies in the eighteenth century attracted the attention of many thoughtful men, but Benjamin Franklin stands practically alone in his effort to explain the phenomenon systematically, in scientific terms. The essay from which the following selection is taken was written as an argument to convince England that there was no need to prohibit manufactures in the colonies, since their population was bound to provide a market that the English factories soon would be unable to supply. Nor was immigration necessary: "natural Generation" could be expected to expand the American population rapidly and indefinitely. Franklin's essay was reprinted many times, both in England and in America; it is known to have influenced the thinking of Thomas Malthus and Frances Place and, probably, Adam Smith.*

✓     ✓     ✓

1. Tables of the Proportion of Marriages to Births, of Deaths to Births, of Marriages to the Number of Inhabitants, &c., form'd on Observations made upon the Bills of Mortality, Christnings, &c., of populous Cities, will not suit Countries, nor will Tables form'd on Observations made on full-settled old Countries, as Europe, suit new Countries, as America.

2. For people increase in Proportion to the Number of Marriages, and that is greater in Proportion to the Ease and Convenience of supporting a Family. When Families can be easily supported, more Persons marry, and earlier in Life.

---

\* Benjamin Franklin, "Observations concerning the Increase of Mankind, Peopling of Countries, &c." Reprinted in *The Papers of Benjamin Franklin*, ed. Leonard W. Labaree, Vol. IV, pp. 227-234. Reproduced by permission of the Yale University Press.

3. In Cities, where all Trades, Occupations, and Offices are full, many delay marrying until they can see how to bear the Charges of a Family; which charges are greater in Cities, as Luxury is more common: many live single during Life, and continue Servants to Families, Journey-men to Trades; &c. hence Cities do not by natural Generation supply themselves with Inhabitants; the Deaths are more than the Births. . . .

5. Europe is generally full settled with Husbandmen, Manufacturers [*laborers*], &c., and therefore cannot now much increase in People: America is chiefly occupied by Indians, who subsist mostly by Hunting. But as the Hunter, of all Men, requires the greatest Quantity of Land from whence to draw his Subsistence, . . . the Europeans found America as fully settled as it well could be by Hunters. . . .

6. Land being thus plenty in America, and so cheap as that a labouring man, that understands Husbandry, can in a short Time save Money enough to purchase a Piece of new Land sufficient for a Plantation, whereon he may subsist a Family, such are not afraid to marry; for, if they even look far enough forward to consider how their Children, when grown up, are to be provided for, they see that more Land is to be had at rates equally easy, all Circumstances considered.

7. Hence Marriages in America are more general, and more generally early, than in Europe. And if it is reckoned there, that there is but one Marriage per Annum among 100 persons, perhaps we may here reckon two; and if in Europe they have but 4 Births to a Marriage (many of their Marriages being late), we may here reckon 8, of which if one half grow up, and own Marriages are made, reckoning one with another at 20 Years of Age, our People must at least be doubled every 20 years.

8. But notwithstanding this Increase, so vast is the Territory of North America, that it will require many Ages to settle it fully; and, till it is fully settled, Labour will never be cheap here, where no Man continues long a Labourer for others, but gets a Plantation of his own, no Man continues long a Journeyman to a Trade, but goes among those new Settlers, and sets up for himself, &c. Hence Labour is no cheaper now in Pennsylvania, than it was 30 Years ago, tho' so many Thousand labouring People have been imported.

9. The Danger therefore of these Colonies interfering with their Mother Country in Trades that depend on Labour, Manufactures, &c., is too remote to require the attention of Great-Britain.

10. But in Proportion to the Increase of the Colonies, a vast Demand is growing for British Manufactures, a glorious Market wholly in the Power of Britain, in which Foreigners cannot

interfere, which will increase in a short Time even beyond her
Power of supplying, tho' her whole Trade should be to her
Colonies: Therefore Britain should not too much restrain Manufactures in her Colonies. A wise and good Mother will not do it.
To distress, is to weaken, and weakening the Children weakens
the whole Family. . . .

22. There is, in short, no Bound to the prolific Nature of
Plants or animals, but what is made by their crowding and
interfering with each other's means of Subsistence. . . . Thus
there are supposed to be now upwards of One Million English
Souls in North-America, (tho' tis thought scarce 80,000 have
been brought over Sea,) and yet perhaps there is not one the
fewer in Britain, but rather many more, on Account of the
Employment the Colonies afford to Manufactures at Home.
This Million doubling, suppose but once in 25 Years, will, in
another Century, be more than the People of England, and the
greatest number of English-men will be on this Side of the
Water. What an Accession of Power to the British Empire by
Sea as well as Land! What Increase of Trade and Navigation!
What Numbers of Ships and Seamen! . . .

# DR. JOHN MORGAN ON THE FUTURE OF SCIENCE IN AMERICA (1765)*

*Dr. John Morgan, a native Philadelphian trained in medicine abroad, was the first professor of medical theory and practice at the College of Philadelphia (later the University of Pennsylvania). He insisted on separating the theory and practice of medicine from both pharmacy and surgery, and he was an enthusiastic prophet of the great development science might expect to enjoy in North America. The following paragraphs from his inaugural address at the College in 1765 express his ideals both as a doctor and as a teacher.*

✓      ✓      ✓

First, I purpose to confine myself, in practice, to those cases which belong most immediately to the office of a Physician. . . . I shall therefore avoid, all I can, interfering in the proper business of surgery, viz. operation. . . .

I am not urging these as arguments for a more expensive practice, but for an improvement of it, by separating physic from surgery and pharmacy, which I think incompatible with them, at least according to the path of education I have followed, by the advice of some of the most eminent and skillful judges of medical science of any in Great Britain. . . .

Medical Science is one whole, of which all the branches I have enumerated are the several parts. They may be considered as the links of a chain that have a mutual connection with one another. Anatomy, Materia Medica, Botany, Chymistry, and the Institutions, are only the ladder by which we are to mount up to practice. A general knowledge, at least, in each one of them, is useful to both Physician and Surgeon; particularly to the former; who in proportion as he is more intimately acquainted with them all, will become more skillful in the healing science. . . .

* John Morgan, *A Discourse upon the Institution of Medical Schools in America* (Philadelphia, 1765), pp. ii, xi, 14, 52-53.

We live on a wide extended continent of which but the smallest portion, even of the inhabited part, has yet been explored. The woods, the mountains, the rivers and bowels of the earth afford ample scope for the reaches of the ingenious. In this respect an American student has some considerable advantages over those of Europe, viz. The most ample field lies before us for the improvement of natural history. The countries of Europe have been repeatedly traversed by numerous persons of the highest genius and learning, intent upon making the strictest search into everything which those countries afford; whence there is less hopes or chance for students who come after them to make new discoveries. This part of the world may be looked upon as offering the richest mines of natural knowledge yet unriffled, sufficient to gratify the laudable thirst of glory in young inquirers into nature. The discovery must greatly enrich medical science, and perpetuate the glory of the authors to latest time. . . .

— Reading No. 15 —

# PROFESSOR JOHN WINTHROP'S EXPLANATION OF EARTHQUAKES*

*John Winthrop IV, Hollis Professor of "Natural Philosophy" at Harvard, made many significant contributions to the history of science in America. One of his contributions was an explanation of the nature of earthquakes, based upon the New England quake of 1755. His statement of the theory that quakes are essentially undulating movements in the earth's crust was relatively new and scientifically sound. It is an example of the careful, original scientific thought, based upon close and accurate observation, that was being done by Americans of the mid-eighteenth century.*

✓        ✓        ✓

Hence it appears, that our buildings were rocked with a kind of angular motion, like that of a cradle; the upper parts of them moving swifter, or thro' greater spaces in the same time than the lower. This perfectly agrees with the idea of an *undulatory* motion of the earth; as you may clearly conceive by turning your thoughts to the case of a vessel floating at rest upon stagnant water, and then suddenly agitated by a great wave rolling under it.

You have now, I suppose, before you the general causes of earthquakes. You have seen that there are in the bowels of the earth inflammable materials, of various kinds, and in large quantities; some in the form of solid or liquid bodies, and others in that of exhalations and vapors; that there are also powerful principles constantly at work, which are capable of enkindling these materials into an actual flame; and that the vapor generated from such flame will endeavour to expand itself on all sides with immense force. If now these inflammable vapors be pent up in close caverns, so as to find no vent till they are collected in large quantity; so soon as they take fire

* John Winthrop, *A Lecture on Earthquakes* (Boston, 1755), pp. 10-11.

in any part, the flame will spread itself, wherever it meets with materials to convey it with as great rapidity, perhaps, as it does in a train of gunpowder; and the vapors produced from hence will rush along through the subterraneous grottos, as they are able to find or force for themselves a passage; and by heaving up the earth that lies over them, will make that kind of progressive swell or *undulation,* in which we have supposed earthquakes commonly to consist; and will at length burst the caverns with a great shaking of the earth, as in springing a mine; and so discharge themselves into the open air.

# — Reading No. 16 —

# BENJAMIN FRANKLIN IDENTIFIES LIGHTNING WITH ELECTRICITY (1749)*

*One of the most brilliant scientific achievements of early American science was Benjamin Franklin's theory and demonstration that lightning is an electrical phenomenon. Franklin first carefully formulated his theory in a paper on "Thunder Gusts" that he sent to Dr. John Mitchell of Virginia in 1749. It was this theory that Franklin tested in his famous kite experiment. It was published in various places and in several languages in Europe; it was this contribution to knowledge, coupled with his other experiments with electricity that were published in Europe at about the same time, that gave Franklin the unchallenged stature of a scientist known and respected throughout the western world.*

      ✓            ✓            ✓

"Observations and Suppositions towards forming a new Hypothesis for explaining the several Phaenomena of Thunder Gusts."

1. Non-Electrical Bodies, that have Electric Fire thrown into [or on] them, will retain it, 'till other Non-electrics, that have less, approach; and then 'tis communicated by a Snap, and becomes equally divided.

2. Electrical Fire loves Water, is strongly attracted by it, and they can subsist together.

3. Air is an Electric per Se, and when dry, will not [readily] conduct the Electrical Fire; it will neither receive it, nor give it to other Bodies; otherwise, no Body surrounded by Air could be electrified positively and negatively: For should it be at-

* Benjamin Franklin, "Observations and Suppositions towards forming a new Hypothesis for explaining the several Phaenomena of Thunder Gusts," *The Papers of Benjamin Franklin,* ed. Leonard W. Labaree, Vol. III, pp. 365-376. Reproduced by permission of Yale University Press.

tempted *positively,* the Air would immediately take away the Overplus; or *negatively,* the Air would supply what was wanting.

4. Water being electrified, the Vapours arising from it will be equally electrified; and floating in the Air, in the Form of Clouds, or otherwise, will retain that Quantity of Electrical Fire, 'till they meet with other Clouds or Bodies not so much electrified; and then will communicate as before mentioned. . . .

9. The Ocean is a Compound of Water a Non-Electric, and Salt an Electric per Se. . . .

27. But Clouds form'd by Vapours, raised from the Sea, having both Fires, and particularly a great Quantity of the Electrical, support their Water Strongly, raise it high; and, being moved by the Winds, may bring it over the Middle of the broadest Continent, from the Middle of the widest Ocean. . . .

32. If a Country be plain, having no Mountains to intercept the electrified Clouds, yet it is not without Means to make them deposite their Water. For if an electrified Cloud, coming from the Sea, meets in the Air a Cloud raised from the Land, and therefore not electrified; the first will flash it's Fire into the latter, and thereby both Clouds shall be made suddenly to deposite Water.

33. The electrified Particles of the first Cloud, close when they lose their Fire: the Particles of the other Cloud close in receiving it: in both they have thereby an Opportunity of Coalescing into Drops. The Concussion, or Jerk, given to the Air, contributes also to shake down the Water; not only from those two Clouds but from others near them. Hence the sudden Fall of Rain immediately after a Flash of Lightning. . . .

39. As Currents of Air, with the Clouds therein, pass different ways, 'tis easy to conceive, how the Clouds passing over each other, may attract each other, and so come near enough for the electrical Stroke; and also how Electrical Clouds may be carried within Land very far from the Sea, before they have an Opportunity to strike. . . .

41. When there is great Heat on the Land in a particular Region, the Sun having shone on it perhaps several Days, while the Surrounding Countries have been screened by Clouds, the lower Air is rarified and rises, the cooler denser Air above descends; the Clouds in that Air meet from all Sides, and joyn over the heated Place; and if some are electrified, others not, Lightning and Thunder succeed, and Showers fall. Hence Gusts after Heats, and cool Air after Gusts; the Water and the Clouds that bring it, coming from a higher and therefore a cooler Region.

42. An Electrical Spark drawn from an irregular Body at some Distance is scarce ever Strait, but shews crooked and

wavering in the Air; So do the Flashes of Lightning; the Clouds being very irregular Bodies.

43. As electrified Clouds pass over a Country, high Hills and high Trees, lofty Towers, Spires, Masts of Ships, Chimneys &c. as so many Prominences and Points, draw the Electrical Fire, and the whole Cloud discharges there.

44. Dangerous therefore is it to take Shelter under a single Tree during a Thunder Gust. It has been fatal to many, both Men and Beasts. . . .

## POPULAR CRITICAL ATTITUDES TOWARD SUPERSTITION AND WITCHCRAFT, ETC.: NATHANIEL AMES IN HIS ALMANAC (1747)*

*A great deal of the scientific knowledge and the rationalism of eighteenth-century science filtered down to the people through the almanacs and the newspapers. One of the healthiest influences exercised by the almanacs upon the popular "mind" of colonial America was the slow but steady corrosion of old superstitions. There was still a good deal of "folk-science" in the almanacs, of course; but the following essay on "conjuration" (witchcraft) that appeared in Nathaniel Ames' Astronomical Diary for 1747 is typical of the sort of intellectual criticism the almanacs were encouraging.*

✓          ✓          ✓

Conjuration, according to Bailey's Definition of the Word, signifys a personal dealing with the Devil, to know any Secret or compass any Design. Many persons in their Study of Nature, have div'd so far above the Apprehension of the Vulgar, that they have been believed to be Necromancers, Magicians, &c. But the Mistake lays in the People's Ignorance, and not in the other Studies. That human Creatures should have actual Society and Communion with spiritual Daemons is a strange Thing. All Men are gaping after Novelties. Our Mathematical Demonstrations please us not so much because our Discoveries are certain, as because they are new. What we know, we slight; and are fond of believing Articles that are most beyond all Belief. They among the Heathen, who made too good a Use of their Reason, to be deceived themselves, were admitted into the Number of holy Sorcerers, as they were called, and made a gainful Market of the Credulity of their Fellow-Creatures. Some

* Nathaniel Ames, *An Astronomical Diary . . . for the Year 1747* (Boston, 1746).

Writings father'd upon Cornelius Agryppa affirm, that if you
call upon Prince Satan by some of his Titles of Honour, in
certain leisure Hours, he'll appear to you with

> Flaming Eyes and Face as black as Soot,
> A Pair of mighty Horns and Cloven foot.

But we are not to believe such Reports, unless the Evidence
of the Truth of the Fact be equal to the Strangeness of the
Thing. — — If there be an old Woman in a Parish prodigious
ugly, her Eyes hollow and red, her Face shrivel'd up, that goes
double, and her Voice trembles, she is a Witch forsooth; but
the handsome young Girls are never suspected; as tho' Satan
took a Delight in the dry Sticks of humane Nature, and would
select the most neglected Creature in the humane Species to
be his Privy-Counsellor.

# REV. CHARLES CHAUNCY ON "REASONABLE RELIGION"*

*The Reverend Charles Chauncy was one of the outstanding liberal Congregational ministers of Boston. Strongly influenced by his reading of the English religious rationalists, he eventually repudiated such ancient Calvinistic doctrines as those of predestination and election. At the same time, his rational approach to religion led him to deplore the apparent abandonment of intelligence and the appeal to elemental emotions that characterized such preachers of the Great Awakening as George Whitefield, Gilbert Tennent, and Jonathan Edwards. This emotionalism was called "enthusiasm." In the sermon cited below, Chauncy warned his people against "enthusiasm" and called upon them to be governed, in their religion, by reason.*

✓            ✓            ✓

1. I am in the first place, to give you some account of enthusiasm. . . .

The word, from its Etymology, carries in it a good meaning, as signifying inspiration from God: in which sense, the prophets under the old testament, and the apostles under the new, might properly be called Enthusiastic. . . .

But the word is more commonly used in a bad sense, as intending an imaginary, not a real inspiration: according to which sense, the Enthusiast is one, who has a conceit of himself as a person favoured with the extraordinary presence of the Deity. He mistakes the workings of his own passions for divine communications, and fancies himself immediately inspired by the Spirit of God when all the while, he is under no other influence than that of an over-heated imagination. . . .

And various are the ways in which their enthusiasm discovers itself. . . .

Sometimes, it affects their bodies, throws them into convul-

* Charles Chauncy, *Enthusiasm described and caution'd against* (Boston, 1742), pp. 1-25.

sions and distortions, into quakings and tremblings. . . . I was myself, when a Lad, an eye-witness to such violent agitations and foamings, in a boisterous female speaker, as I could not behold but with surprize and wonder. . . .

Sometimes, it appears in their imaginary peculiar intimacy with heaven. They are, in their own opinion, the special favourites of God, have more familiar converse with him than other good men, and receive immediately extraordinary communications from him. The tho'ts, which suddenly rise up in their minds, they take for suggestions of the Spirits; their very fancies are divine illuminations; nor are they strongly inclin'd to any thing, but 'tis an impulse from God, a plain revelation of his will. . . .

But in nothing does the enthusiasm of these persons discover it self more, than in the disregard they express to the Dictates of reason. . . .

But as the most suitable guard against the first tendencies toward enthusiasm, let me recommend to you the following words of counsel.

1. Get a true understanding of the proper work of the Spirit, and don't place it in those things wherein the gospel does not make it to consist. . . .

2. Keep close to the Scriptures, and admit of nothing for an impression of the Spirit, but what agrees with that unerring rule. . . .

3. Make use of the Reason and Understanding God has given you. . . . Next to the Scripture, there is no greater enemy to enthusiasm, than reason. . . .

4. You must not lay too great stress upon the workings of your passions and affections. . . .

5. In the last place here, you must not forget to go to God by prayer. . . .

There is such a thing as real religion, let the conduct of men be what it will; and tis, in it's nature, a sober, calm, reasonable thing: Nor is it an objection of any weight against the sobriety or reasonableness of it, that there have been enthusiasts, who have acted as tho' it was a wild, imaginary business. . . . We shou'd rather judge of it from the conduct of men of a sound judgment; whose lives have been such a uniform, beautiful transcript of that which is just and good, that we can't but think well of religion, as display'd in their example.

# REV. JONATHAN DICKINSON ON CALVINISTIC ORTHODOXY IN AMERICA*

*The Reverend Jonathan Dickinson was one of the most distinguished theologians in the colonies. Indeed, his colleague, Thomas Foxcroft, who wrote the preface to the doctrinal statement from which the following selection is taken, said that Dickinson's explanation of the basic positions of (Calvinistic) Christianity was the best that had even been written in America. Dickinson's position was thoroughly orthodox: the eternal and absolute nature of God, salvation by election, predestination, eternal happiness for the elect, eternal hell for the damned, and so on.*

✓          ✓          ✓

That there is a supream and eternal Being, and that he is possess'd of all infinite Perfections, are Truths so visible by the Light of Nature; that to call these into Question is not only Weakness and Ignorance; but the Height of Stupidity and Madness. . . . We have clear Light to discover that he is, and that he is infinite; yet none but his own infinite Mind can fully understand what he is, or how he exists. . . . [*As corollaries of the absolute nature of God, he notes:*]

1. The Eternity of God's lasting love. Before the Foundation of the World.

2. Here is set in View the Object of the Decree of Election. . . . And as all the children of God, and none but they, shall inherit eternal Life, so all that shall inherit eternal Life, and none but they, were predestined to the Adoption of Children.

3. . . . They are chosen in him; and predestined to the adoption of children by Jesus Christ. . . .

5. The only Motive (if I may so speak) by which God was

* Jonathan Dickinson, *The True Scripture-Doctrine Concerning Some Important Points of the Christian Faith* (Boston, 1741), pp. 1-5.

acted in the Decree of Election. According to the good Pleasure of his Will. He was himself his own Motive and End. As there was nothing eternally existing but God; so there could be nothing out[side] of himself to influence his eternal Counsels. . . . Thus I have given a brief and general View of the Words before us; and shall now endeavour a more distinct consideration of them under these Propositions.

1. That God has according to the good Pleasure of his Will, from all Eternity, elected some to everlasting Life.

2. All that God has elected, are chosen to Salvation by and through the Lord Jesus Christ.

3. All who are thus chosen to Salvation, shall be sanctified and made meet to partake of it. . . .

# JONATHAN EDWARDS' PHILOSOPHY OF RELIGION*

*Jonathan Edwards, minister of the Congregational church at Northampton, Massachusetts, was unquestionably one of the greatest religious thinkers ever to appear in America. While he is usually thought of as a preacher of the Great Awakening, Edwards formulated a genuinely intellectual explanation of the central place of the emotions in religion. His philosophy of religion was an integral part—and the logical apex—of his philosophy of existence, as described in Chapter 6. The universe revealed by science was real, he thought. Man, as a natural creature, was characterized by certain qualities, including the emotions, which were given him by God (of whose mind the entire natural universe was a vast manifestation) as a natural mechanism for coming into rapport with God himself. For this reason, the emotions must be appealed to in the effort to bring the Christian sinner to a sense of the beauty of God and of his own dependence upon him. In his own way, then, Edwards brought the emotions and reason together in the soul; for him, there could be no conflict.*

1   1   1

Such seems to be our nature, and such the laws of the union of soul and body, that there never is in any case whatsoever, any lively and vigorous exercise of the will or inclination of the soul, without some effect upon the body, in some alteration of the motion of its fluids, and especially of the animal spirits. And, on the other hand, from the same laws of the union of the soul and body, the constitution of the body, and the motion of its fluids, may promote the exercise of the affections. But yet it is not the body, but the mind only, that is the proper

---

* Jonathan Edwards, "Concerning the Nature of the Affections, and Their Importance to Religion," *The Works of President Edwards* (4 vols., New York, 1847), Vol. III, pp. 4-21.

seat of the affections. The body of man is no more capable of being really the subject of love or hatred, joy or sorrow, fear or hope, than the body of a tree, or than the same body of man is capable of thinking and understanding. As it is the soul only that has ideas, so it is the soul only that is pleased or displeased with its ideas. As it is the soul only that thinks, so it is the soul only that loves or hates, rejoices or is grieved at what it thinks of. Nor are these motions of the animal spirits, and fluids of the body, any thing properly belonging to the nature of the affections, though they always accompany them, in the present state; but are only effects or concomitants of the affections that are entirely distinct from the affections themselves, and no way essential to them; so that an unbodied spirit may be as capable of love and hatred, joy or sorrow, hope or fear, or other affections, as one that is united to a body. . . .

God has given to mankind affections, for the same purpose which he has given all the faculties and principles of the human soul for, viz., that they might be subservient to man's chief end, and the great business for which God has created him, that is, the business of religion. And yet how common is it among mankind, that their affections are much more exercised and engaged in other matters, than in religion!

# WILLIAM LIVINGSTON ON RELIGIOUS TOLERATION IN AMERICA*

*William Livingston was an outstanding liberal lawyer and political leader in New York about the middle of the eighteenth century. A brilliant essayist, he contributed a number of essays on religious freedom, freedom of the press, and education to the famous* Independent Reflector. *The following selection is from a separately published "address" to Sir Charles Hardy on the subject of religious toleration, which he describes as one of the typical characteristics of American colonial society.*

✦          ✦          ✦

Our religious character, is as multiform, as our origin is various. Popery however, is not to be enumerated among our several professions. We equally detest the doctrines, and the interests of Rome. With the same passion for Freedom, so strongly apparent, in our secular concerns, are we also inspired in matters of religion. And different as our sentiments are on that momentous subject, (bating [*excepting*] a few, whose fondness for the English hierarchy, inclines them to wish for what they would perhaps, be the first to deplore) we universally concur, in an aversion to ecclesiastical establishments. This levelling principle, as some are pleased most improperly to stile it, is no innovation, in our colony constitution, but rather, one of its original and fundamental ingredients. It is a principle, to which we owe our numbers,—our prosperity,—our opulence. A principle indispensibly requisite, in the formation of every infant state: A principle in fine, chiefly adverted to, in the capitulation and surrender of this province by the Dutch [*1664*]; and in the conditions upon which it was settled, by the Duke of York: The latter, expressly declaring, "that every township, shall pay their own minister, according to such agreement, as they shall make with him; the ministers being elected, by the

* William Livingston, *An Address to His Excellency Sir Charles Hardy* (New York, 1755), pp. vii-viii.

major part of the householders and inhabitants of the town."
And let me humbly presume, to assure your Excellency, that
nothing is more odious to the people, who have the honour to
be governed by you, than religious tests, and discriminations,
for civil purposes. Tests and discriminations, so expressly repugnant, to the very genius of our provincial constitution. . . .

# CADWALLADER COLDEN'S DEISTIC PHILOSOPHY*

*Cadwallader Colden, doctor, politician, and scientist, was one of the outstanding intellectuals in the colonies. He did a great deal of scientific observation and experimentation, but his major intellectual efforts were devoted to the formulation of a scientific philosophy (which he never completed) of material existence. He tended to be a pure materialist in his philosophy, but a correspondence with Dr. Samuel Johnson, the idealist philosopher, convinced him that he must take cognizance of some over-all directing intelligence in the universe, separate from matter. This placed him, logically, among the Deists. The following selection, taken from his* The Principles of Action in Matter, *expresses the gist of his thought on this problem.*

✦ ✦ ✦

1. The elementary parts of matter, or the smallest parts of which matter is supposed or imagined to be compounded, must have one single simple action, for it cannot be imagined that a complication of different actions can arise from one simple uncompounded thing. . . .

2. The elementary parts of matter act uniformly, necessarily and invariably, always in the same manner, and with the same degree of force.

3. Nothing in the action of matter can induce one to think that its action proceeds from any sense, perception, intelligence or will, or that sense or will can be essential to matter, or that they are naturally involved or complicated with the actions of matter: for our ideas of the action of matter are perfect and compleat, though it were supposed that sense, perception, intelligence or will, existed no where but in ourselves.

* Cadwallader Colden, *The Principles of Action in Matter, The Gravitation of Bodies, and The Motions of the Planets, Explained from those Principles* (London, 1751), pp. 157-167.

4. Then since we cannot doubt of the existence of sense of perception, intelligence and will, they must be the action, operation, or properties of some kind of being distinct from what is commonly called matter. . . .

9. All these discover foresight, design, and purpose, of which innumerable other instances may be given, in every part of the universe that comes within our knowledge. The more knowledge we have of anything, the more intelligence we discover in its formation; . . . .

10. It follows then, that the first formation of all kinds of material systems, the greatest and the least, was made by some intelligent being; that some being form'd the grand solar system, the more particular system of this earth, and all the small systems on it, whether animal, vegetable, or mineral, each according to its nature, as is most conducive for the well-being of every individual, and of the universal system of nature.

13. The actions of intelligent beings cannot be the object of mathematical inquiry. . . . Therefore any inquiry into the actions of an intelligent agent must be on different principles, from what are used in an inquiry into the actions of matter. . . .

19. Nature, or more properly speaking, the infinite intelligent Archeus, has ordered so, that, since the several individual systems must in time fail, from their natural constitution, this defeat is supplied by the generation of new and similar systems, the constant method of doing which is by fermentation, under the direction of the intelligent agent. . . .

# SAMUEL JOHNSON'S IDEALISM: THE IDEAS OF THINGS AS THE ONLY REALITY*

*Samuel Johnson, president of King's College in New York, was one of the few formal philosophers in colonial America. He was a follower of Berkeley, Anglican Bishop of Cloyne, who was the founder of eighteenth-century idealism. The idealists, starting from Locke's demonstration that all knowledge is derived from sensory impressions, argued very plausibly that since all knowledge of the objective world was subjective— that is, inside the brain of the individual person—it was the internal, subjective ideas of things that constituted the only provable reality. Further, they believed that, as Johnson says, these ideas of things derive "from the universal presence and action of the Deity."*

5. Our minds may be said to be created mere *tabulae rasae;* they have no notices of any object of any kind properly created in them, or created with them: yet I apprehend, that in all the notices, they have of any kind of objects, they have an immediate dependence upon the Deity, as really as they depend upon Him for their existence; i.e., they are no more authors to themselves of the objects of their perceptions, or the light by which they perceive them, than of the power of perceiving itself; but that they perceive them by a perpetual intercourse with that great Parent Mind, to whose incessant agency they are entirely passive, both in all the perceptions of sense, and in all that intellectual light by which they perceive the objects of the pure intellect. . . .

* Samuel Johnson, *Elementa Philosophica,* reprinted in *Samuel Johnson, President of King's College: His Career and Writings* (4 vols., New York: Columbia University Press, 1929), Vol. II, pp. 374-380. Reproduced by permission of the Columbia University Press.

In the perception of these ideas of objects of sense, we find our minds are merely passive, it not being in our power . . . whether we will see light and colors, hear sounds, etc. We are not causes to ourselves of these perceptions, nor can they be produced in our minds without a cause. . . .

8. These ideas on objects of sense are commonly supposed to be pictures or representations of things without us, and indeed external to any mind, even that of the Deity himself, and the truth or reality of them is conceived to consist in their being exact pictures of things or objects without us, which are supposed to be the real things. But as it is impossible for us to perceive what is without our minds, and consequently, what those supposed originals are, and whether these ideas of ours are just resemblances of them or not; I am afraid this notion of them will lead us into an inextricable skepticism. I am therefore apt to think that these ideas, or immediate objects of sense, are the real things, at least all that we are concerned with, I mean, of the sensible kind; and that the reality of them consists in their stability and consistence, or their being, in a stable manner, exhibited to our minds, or produced in them, and in a steady connection with each other, conformable to certain fixed laws of nature, which the great Father of Spirits hath established to himself, according to which he constantly operates and affects our minds, and from which He will not vary, unless upon extraordinary occasions, as in the case of miracles. . . .

14. Now if it be asked, whence does this light derive, whereby all created minds at once perceive, as by a common standard, the same things alike to be true and right. I answer, I have no other way to conceive how I come to be affected with this intuitive intellectual light, whereof I am conscious, than by deriving it from the universal presence and action of the Deity, or a perpetual communication with the great father of lights, or rather his eternal word and spirit, exhibiting and impressing. . . .

## JONATHAN EDWARDS' IDEALISM: THE PERCEPTION OF SPIRITUAL THINGS BY THE "SENSE OF THE HEART"*

*Jonathan Edwards, certainly the most powerful philosophical mind in eighteenth-century America, constructed a philosophical synthesis of the material universe revealed by science and the spiritual reality that was God. For him, there was no real dichotomy between matter and spirit; all things exist as manifestations of the mind of God. And yet there is a difference between material phenomena and spiritual phenomena within this monistic concept of reality. Starting from Locke, Edwards explained that while men perceive the gross material things with the senses of touch, taste, smell, sight, and hearing, they perceive spiritual phenomena, such as "beauty and deformity, or loveliness and hatefulness, and all ideas of delight or comfort, and pleasure of body or mind" by an inward sense, which he calls the "sense of the heart." This is the sense by which men perceive the reality of God; this inward perceptive sense is just as real and just as important as the other senses—perhaps more important. This epistemological explanation of men's spiritual knowledge, an elaboration of an idea suggested by Locke, was essential to Edwards' logical explanation of reality and man's relationship to it.*

ᛨ       ᛨ       ᛨ

Hence arises another great distinction of the kind of understanding of mental things that appertain or relate to spiritual beings, which is somewhat diverse from the former, viz. of speculative and sensible, or

1. That understanding which consists in mere SPECULATION, or the understanding of the Head; or

* Perry Miller, ed., "Jonathan Edwards on the Sense of the Heart," *The Harvard Historical Review,* Vol. XLI, No. 2 (April, 1948), pp. 136-137. Reproduced by permission of the editor and *Harvard Historical Review.*

2. That which consists in the SENSE OF THE HEART.

The former includes all that understanding that is without any proper ideal apprehension or view, or all understanding of mental things of either faculty, that is only by signs, and also all ideal views of things that are merely intellectual, or appertain only to the faculty of understanding; i.e. all that understanding of things, that does not consist in, or imply, some motion of the will, or in other words (to speak figuratively) some feeling of the heart, is mere speculative knowledge, whether it be an ideal apprehension of them, or no.

But all that understanding of things, that does consist in, or involve, such a sense or feeling, is not merely speculative, but sensible knowledge. So is all ideal apprehension of beauty and deformity, or loveliness and hatefulness, and all ideas of delight or comfort, and pleasure of body or mind, and pain, trouble, or misery, and all ideal apprehension of desires and longings, esteem, acquiescence, hope, fear, contempt, choosing, refusing, accepting, rejecting, loving, hating, anger, and the idea of all the affections of the minds, and all their motions and exercises, and all ideal views of dignity, or excellency of any kind, and also all ideas of terrible greatness, or awful majesty, meanness or contemptibleness, value and importance. All knowledge of this sort, as it is of things that concern the heart, or the will and affections, so it all relates to the good or evil which the sensible knowledge of things this nature involves; and nothing is called sensible knowledge upon any other account but the sense, or kind of inward tasting or feeling, of sweetness or pleasure, bitterness or pain, that is implied in it, or arises from it. Yet it is not only the mere ideal apprehension of that good or evil that is included in what is [*called*] being sensible; but also the ideal apprehensions of other things that appertain to the things known, on which the goodness or evil that attends them depends. As for instance, some men are said to have a sense of the dreadfulness of God's displeasure. This apprehension of God's displeasure is called having a sense, and is to be looked upon as a part of sensible knowledge, because of the evil or pain in the object of God's displeasure, that is connected with that displeasure. But yet in a sense of the terribleness of God's displeasure there is implied an ideal apprehension of more things than merely of that pain or misery or sense of God's heart: there is implied an ideal apprehension of the being of God, as of some intellectual existence, and an ideal apprehension of his greatness and of the greatness of his power. . . .

# BENJAMIN FRANKLIN'S REJECTION OF METAPHYSICS

*Benjamin Franklin was a man of eminently practical mind. As he says, after certain youthful experiments with metaphysical thinking he repudiated metaphysics, and he tended, consistently through the rest of his life, to test the validity of all customs, institutions, and ideas pragmatically by their beneficial or harmful effects on human happiness. The first of the following paragraphs is taken from a letter he wrote (it is supposed) to Thomas Hopkinson;\* the second is from his autobiography, written retrospectively late in his life.†*

✓      ✓      ✓

(a) Shall I hazard a Thought to you [*that?*] for aught I know is new, viz. If God was before all Things, and fill'd all Space; then, when he form'd what we call Matter, he must have done it out of his own Thinking immaterial Substance. The same, tho' he had not fill'd all Space; if it be true that *Ex nihilo nihil fit* [*nothing is made from nothing*]. From hence may we not draw this Conclusion, That if any Part of Matter does not at present act and think, 'tis not from an Incapacity in its Nature [*but from*] a positive Restraint. I know not yet [*what other*] Consequences may follow the admitting of [*this position*] and therefore I will not be oblig'd to defend it. . . . The great Uncertainty I have found in that Science; the wide Contradictions and endless Disputes it affords; and the horrible Errors I led my self into when a young Man, by drawing a Chain of plain Consequences as I thought them, from true

---

\* (a) Franklin to [Thomas Hopkinson?], [October, 1746], *The Papers of Benjamin Franklin,* ed. Leonard W. Labaree, Vol. III, pp. 84-89. Reproduced by permission of Yale University Press.

† (b) Benjamin Franklin, *The Autobiography of Benjamin Franklin,* ed. Nathan C. Goodman (New York: Carlton House, 1932), pp. 62-63.

Principles, have given me a Disgust to what I was once extremly fond of.

(b) I grew convinc'd that truth, sincerity and integrity in dealings between man and man were of the utmost importance to the felicity of life; and I formed written resolutions, which still remain in my journal book, to practice them ever while I lived. Revelation had indeed no weight with me, as such; but I entertain'd an opinion that, though certain actions might not be bad because they were forbidden by it, or good because it commanded them, yet probably these actions might be forbidden because they were bad for us, or commanded because they were beneficial to us, in their own natures, all the circumstances being considered. And this persuasion, with the kind hand of Providence, or some guardian angel, or accidental favoring circumstances and situations, or all together, preserved me, thro this dangerous time of youth, and the hazardous situations I was sometimes in among strangers, remote from the eye and advice of my father, without any gross immorality or injustice, that might have been expected from my want of religion. . . .

## — Reading No. 26 —

## THE INDIAN TREATY AS LITERATURE: THE TREATY OF LANCASTER (1744)*

*In the conferences between the leaders of the English colonies and Indian chieftains representing their tribes, called "treaties," the communication of ideas took place in an idiom that was neither purely Indian nor purely English, but a synthesis of both. The Indian chiefs spoke in their native languages; the English leaders spoke English; the speeches of each would be translated to the other by interpreters who were often themselves half-breeds. The Indians, of course, spoke out of a culture that was almost entirely innocent of European influences. Their speeches, even as they emerged from the translations of the interpreters, were couched in the Indians' own style and rich in the imagery and symbolisms of the Indian mind. The white speakers, in their effort to speak in terms the Indians could understand, deliberately imitated the Indian imagery and symbolism, even the Indian style. The outcome, as literature, was a primitive genre that richly expressed the conflicts and the agreements, the frictions and the values that sprang from the experiences involved in the contact of the two cultures. The following paragraphs are taken from the Treaty of Lancaster, Pennsylvania, held in 1744.*

✓        ✓        ✓

*The Speech of Gachradodow, June 30, 1744*

Brother Assaragoa [*the Governor of Virginia*],

The World at the first was made on the other Side of the great Water different from what it was on this Side, as may be known from the different Colours of our Skin, and of our Flesh, and that which you call Justice may not be so amongst us; you have your Laws and Customs, and so have we. The Great King might send you over to conquer the Indians, but

* *A Treaty, Held at the Town of Lancaster, in Pennsylvania, . . . with the Indians of the Six Nations, in June, 1744* (Philadelphia, 1744), pp. 23, 35-37.

it looks to us that God did not approve of it; if he had, he would not have placed the Sea where it is, as the Limit between us and you.

Brother Assaragoa,

Tho' great Things are well remembered among us, yet we don't remember that we were ever conquered by the Great King, or that we have been employed by the Great King to conquer others; if it was so, it is beyond our Memory. We do remember that we were employed by Maryland to conquer the Conestogoes, and that the second time we were at War with them, we carried them all off. . . .

✓          ✓          ✓

*The Speech of Conassatego, July 4, 1744*

Brother Assaragoa,

You told us . . . you had a great House provided for the Education of Youth, and that there were several White People and Indian Children there to learn Languages, and to write and read, and invited us to send some of our Children amongst you, etc.

We must let you know we love our Children too well to send them so great a Way, and the Indians are not inclined to give their children Learning. We allow it to be good, and we thank you for your Invitation; but our Customs differing from yours, you will be so good as to excuse us. . . .

Brother Tocarry-Logan [*Governor of Maryland*],

You told us Yesterday, that since there was now nothing in Controversy between us, and the Affair of the Land was settled to your Satisfaction, you would now brighten the Chain of Friendship which hath subsisted between you and us ever since we became Brethren; we are well pleased with the Proposition, and we thank you for it; we also are inclined to renew all Treaties, and keep a good correspondence with you. You told us further, if ever we perceived the chain had contracted any Rust, to let you Know, and you would take care to take the Rust out, and preserve it bright. We agree with you in this, and shall, on our Parts, do every thing to preserve a good Understanding, and to live in the same Friendship with you as with our Brother Orcas and Assaragoa; in Confirmation whereof, we give you this Belt of Wampum.

On which the usual Cry of Yo-hah was given.

## — Reading No. 27 —

## INTERNATIONAL HATRED IN LITERATURE: "GALLIC PERFIDY," BY JOHN MAYLEM (1758)*

*John Maylem was a young poet of Newport, Rhode Island, at the time of the Seven Years War, and was taken as a prisoner of war by the French and Indians at the surrender of Fort William Henry. He never lived to realize the promise of his youth, but many of the poems that he wrote display the fear, the distrust, the religious antagonisms, and the nationalistic hatred felt by most, probably, of the Angloamericans toward their French neighbors. The following selection, from Maylem's poem "Gallic Perfidy," is a good example of the feelings that Maylem shared with so many of his fellow Americans.*

Who, of late, in Epic Strains essay'd,
And sung the Hero on *Acadie's* Plains;
Dreadful in Arms, and Vest of Tyrian Hue,
With Laurel-Wreath, and mighty Conquest crown'd,
In equal Numbers still attempt to sing;
But yet in rougher strain, for softer Rhyme
Seems not adapt to this my solemn Theme.
Not how the Gaul and swarthy Foe approach'd
And first assail'd the Fortress; nor what pass'd
In the dread Interval of eight Days Siege:
I mean to sing but Breach of plighted Faith,
And violation of the sacred Laws
Of Nature and of Nations; with th'Event,
The dire Event and fatal Consequence,
Attendant on the Foes perfidious Breach
Of solemn and capitulated Terms.

* John Maylem, *Gallic Perfidy* (Boston, 1758).

Amazing Perfidy! — — — — — — — — —
— — — — — — — — — — — Not to invoke
A vulgar Muse.— Ye Powers of Fury lend
Some mighty Phrensy to enrage my Breast
With solemn Song, beyond All Nature's Strain!
For such the Scene of which I mean to sing.
Enough! I rave! —the Furies rack my Brain!
I feel their Influence now inspire my Song!
My lab'ring Muse dwells with the raving God!
I feel him here! my head turns round! 'twill burst!
So have I seen a Bomb, with livid Train,
(Emitted from a Mortar) big with Death,
And fraught, full fraught with Hell's Combustibles,
Lay dreadful on the Ground; then with a Force
Stupendous, shiver in a thousand Atoms! . . .

For now behold Hell's swarthy Allies dire,
With Visage foul, and horrid awful Grin;
Red, black, and green besmear'd their mighty Fronts;
With snaky Braids, and dreadful Ornament,
And pitchy Feathers platted on their Hair;
Obscene and naked, daub'd with various Paints,
With Aspect dire, and full *Canadian* Rage,
And murd'rous Shafts (Presage of awful Death!)
Like Fiends of Hell, or worse (if possible)
With fearful Yell, to raise the Hell below,
To the Assistance of the Hell within 'em,
Rush on their unforewarn'd defenceless Prey. . . .

# REV. MATHER BYLES ON "BOMBASTIC AND GRUBSTREET STYLE" (1745)*

*The Reverend Mather Byles was an eighteenth-century member of the famous Mather "dynasty" of Congregationalist divines. But Byles showed considerable individuality on several literary counts: he was a poet who often wrote on secular subjects; he was a humorist of no mean gifts, especially as a punster; and he was a literary critic who ridiculed the formal, "bombastic" style of his literary ancestors. He himself was devoted to a simple literary style; in this he was typical of the stylistic moods of his time. The paragraphs below are taken from his famous essay on "Bombastic and Grubstreet Style," published in 1745.*

✓      ✓      ✓

There have been innumerable Authors, from *Aristotle's Rhetorick* to *Longinus's Treatise of the Sublime,* and from thence down to the Compiler of our modern *Horn-book,* who have written Introductions to the Art of Polite Writing. Every one that can just distinguish his Twenty Four Letters sets up for a Judge of it; as all who are able to flourish a Goose's Quill, pretend to be Masters of that Secret. . . . To conclude, the Science of correct Writing having been a Subject exhausted by so many able Hands, and seeing all the Rabble of Scriblers are such indisputable Proficients in it; not to mention my own Incapacity for such an Undertaking; I shall not be so vain as to offer my Thoughts upon it: But I shall apply my Labours at this Time, to an Ornament of a contrary Nature, which is a Theme intirely New, Namely, The Art of writing Incorrectly. . . .

Authors of this Kind may be divided into two Classes, generally known under the Denomination of the Bombastick and

* Mather Byles, "Bombastic and Grubstreet Style: A Satire," *The American Magazine and Historical Chronicle* (Boston), January, 1745, pp. 1-4.

the Grubstreet. The latter of these Characters is easily attained, provided a Man can but keep himself from thinking, and yet so contrive Matters, as to let his Pen run along unmolested over a Sheet of White Paper, and drop a convenient Quantity of Words, at proper Intervals on it. A Person who is acquainted with this Secret, may, with great Facility and Composure of Mind, furnish himself with a comfortable Stock of Reputation, as often as he finds it requisite. . . .

I shall, perhaps, dedicate some future Essay to the In-couragement of these worthy Gentlemen, but at this Time I intend to consider those my ingenious Fellow-Labourers, who deviate into the contrary Extream; I mean the Admirers of Bombast and Fustian. . . .

A Friend of mine who writes in this exorbitant Style, Mr. Richard Stentor by Name, shall be the Hero of the present Essay. Mr. Stentor as to his exterior Figure, is one of the portliest Mortals that have flourished in our World, since Goliath over-top'd the Philistian Army. He is moderately speaking, Nine Foot high, and Four in Diameter. His Voice is not unlike the Roar and Rapidity of a Torrent foaming down a Mountain, and reverberated amongst the neighbouring Rocks. The Hurry of Vociferation with which he drives along in the Heat of an Argument, imitates the Thunder of a Cart-load of Stones poured out upon a Pavement. He was educated in a Ship of War, and one would imagine he learnt the Notes of his Gamut, from the various Whistlings of a Tempest thro' the Rigging of his Vessel. I was once so unadvised as to offer my Dissent from one of his opinions; but I had better have held my Tongue: He turned upon me, and rung me such a Peal of Eloquence, that had I not made off with the greatest Precipitation, would have gone near to have stun'd, and made me deaf all my Days. Nay, I have cause to think my Hearing has been never the better for it to this Moment. . . .

# DRAMATIC CRITICISM IN PHILADELPHIA (1758)*

*There was not much theatrical activity in the colonies before the American Revolution, and there was even less dramatic writing. There was some of both, however, and New York, Philadelphia, Williamsburg, and Charleston were its chief centers. Almost as soon as there were plays, too, there was dramatic criticism. The following review, one of the earliest in the colonies, was published in* The American Magazine *(Philadelphia) in 1758.*

✓      ✓      ✓

The piece in general, whatever may be its defects, abounds with warm and generous sentiments of liberty and public spirit, and the applause with which it has been received is therefore a proof that these principles are still alive among us. There is also one passage, which, in a few words, more strongly recommends religion as a principle of heroic actions than the most elaborate reasoning or florid declamation. Lysander when he is alone and in prison, expecting every moment to die by the hand of the executioner, falls in to a very natural and important series of reflection[s] concerning the immortality of his soul; the reasons for and against it seem to be nearly equiponderate, but at last he comes to this resolution,

"While I live I'll act as if I were immortal."

This sentence includes at once all the force of precept and example, as it represents a man who doubts of his immortality, determining that to act nobly he must act as if he were immortal. Such a proof, that to act as an infidel is to act basely, reaches at once the understanding and the heart, and was ap-

* "The Story of Ages, a new Tragedy, with Critical Remarks," *The American Magazine,* Vol. I, No. IX (June, 1758), pp. 416-417.

plauded with a zeal that did equal honour to the author, the actor, and the audience. . . .

The execution of this play is unequal, some very fine strokes of poetry and the flattest prose, being frequently found in the very same speeches and sentences. . . .

# BENJAMIN FRANKLIN'S IDEAS ON EDUCATION (1749)*

*Benjamin Franklin was the clearest and most systematic thinker about education in colonial America, although there were many distinguished thinkers in this field. Franklin's thought was typical of the widespread secularizing tendency in education, with its emphasis upon the teaching of "practical" subjects, the English language, and the civic virtues. Franklin was largely responsible for the establishment of the Philadelphia Academy, under the presidency of William Smith, which attempted to put his ideas into practice.*

It has long been regretted as a Misfortune to the Youth of this Province, that we have no Academy, in which they might receive the Accomplishments of a regular Education. . . .

The good Education of Youth has been esteemed by wise Men in all Ages, as the surest Foundation of the Happiness both of private Families and of Common-wealths. Almost all Governments have therefore made it a principal Object of their Attention, to establish and endow with proper Revenues, such Seminaries of Learning, as might supply the succeeding Age with Men qualified to serve the Publick with Honour to themselves, and to their Country.

Many of the first Settlers of these Provinces, were Men who had received a good Education in Europe, and to their Wisdom and good Management we owe much of our present Prosperity. But their Hands were full, and they could not do all Things. The present Race are not thought to be generally of equal Ability: For though the American Youth are allow'd not to

* Benjamin Franklin, *Proposals Relating to the Education of Youth in Pensilvania* (Philadelphia, 1749). Reprinted *in The Papers of Benjamin Franklin,* ed. Leonard W. Labaree, Vol. III, pp. 397-419. Reproduced by permission of Yale University Press.

want Capacity; yet the best Capacities require Cultivation, it being truly with them, as with the best Ground, which unless well tilled and sowed with profitable Seed, produces only ranker Weeds. . . .

As to their Studies, it would be well if they could be taught every Thing that is useful, and every Thing that is ornamental: But Art is long, and their Time is short. It is therefore propos'd that they learn those Things that are likely to be most useful and most ornamental, Regard being had to the several Professions for which they are intended.

All should be taught to write a fair Hand, and swift, as that is useful to All. And with it may be learnt something of Drawing, by Imitation of Prints, and some of the first Principles of Perspective.

Arithmetick, Accounts, and some of the first Principles of Geometry and Astronomy.

The English Language might be taught by Grammar; in which some of our best Writers, as Tillotson, Addison, Pope, Algernon Sidney, Cato's Letters, &c. should be Classicks: The Stiles principally to be cultivated, being the clear and the concise. Reading should also be taught, and pronouncing, properly, distinctly, emphatically; not with an even Tone, which underdoes, nor a theatrical, which over-does Nature. . . .

But if History be made a constant Part of their Reading, such as the Translations of the Greek and Roman Historians, and the modern Histories of antient Greece and Rome, &c. may not almost all Kinds of useful Knowledge be that Way introduc'd to Advantage, and with Pleasure to the Student? . . .

History will also give Occasion to expatiate on the Advantage of Civil Orders and Constitutions, how Men and their Properties are protected by joining in Societies and establishing Government; their Industry encouraged and rewarded, Arts invented, and Life made more comfortable: The Advantages of Liberty, Mischiefs of Licentiousness, Benefits arising from good Laws and a due Execution of Justice, &c. Thus may the first Principles of sound Politicks be fix'd in the minds of Youth. . . .

If the new Universal History were also read, it would give a connected Idea of human Affairs, so far as it goes, which should be follow'd by the best modern Histories, particularly of our Mother Country; then of these Colonies; which should be accompanied with Observations on their Rise, Encrease, Use to Great-Britain, Encouragements, Discouragements, &c. the Means to make them flourish, secure their Liberties, &c. . . .

While they are reading Natural History [*science*], might not a little Gardening, Planting, Grafting, Inoculating, &c. be taught and practised; and now and then Excursions made to the neighbouring Plantations of the best Farmers, their Methods observ'd and reason'd upon for the Information of Youth. The Improvement of Agriculture being useful to all, and Skill in it no Disparagement to any.

The History of Commerce, of the Invention of Arts, Rise of Manufactures, Progress of Trade, Change of its Seats, with the Reasons, Causes, &c. may also be made entertaining to Youth, and will be useful to all. . . . This will be the Time to show them Prints of antient and modern Machines, to explain them, to let them be copied, and to give Lectures in Mechanical Philosophy. . . .

The Idea of what is true Merit, should also be often presented to Youth, explain'd and impress'd on their Minds, as consisting in an Inclination join'd with an Ability to serve Mankind, one's Country, Friends and Family; which Ability is (with the Blessing of God) to be acquir'd or greatly encreas'd by true Learning; and should indeed be the great Aim and End of all Learning.

## — Reading No. 31 —

## ANDREW HAMILTON ON THE FREEDOM OF THE PRESS (1734)*

*The most famous pronouncement of the doctrine of the freedom of the press was that made by Andrew Hamilton, counsel for John Peter Zenger, publisher of* The New York Weekly Journal, *at Zenger's trial for libel in 1734. Hamilton was a well-known lawyer of Philadelphia who traveled to New York for Zenger's defense. This famous speech to the jury was successful in winning Zenger's acquittal, but it had little immediate effect upon the laws limiting the activities of printing establishments. Its greatest significance lies in the fact that it represented the thinking of many leaders in colonial America at the time, thinking that may be said to have preceded the later— much later—liberalization of the law.*

✓    ✓    ✓

There is heresy in law, as well as in religion, and both have changed very much; and we well know, that it is not two centuries ago that a man would have been burnt as an heretic, for owning such opinions in matters of religion as are publicly wrote and printed at this day. . . . It is agreed upon by all men that this is a reign of liberty, and while men keep within the bounds of truth, I hope they may with safety both speak and write their sentiments of the conduct of men in power, I mean of that part of their conduct only, which affects the liberty or property of the people under their administration. Were this to be denied, then the next step may make them slaves; for what notions can be entertained of slavery, beyond that of suffering the greatest injuries and oppressions, without

* P. Radin, ed., *The Trial of John Peter Zenger (1734) and the Freedom of the Press* (Sutro Branch, California State Library, Occasional Papers, English Series, No. 7. San Francisco: California State Library, 1940), pp. 43-55. Reprinted by permission of the Sutro Branch of the California State Library.

the liberty of complaining; or if they do, to be destroyed, body and estate, for so daring. . . .

The loss of liberty to a generous mind, is worse than death; and yet we know there have been those, in all ages, who, for the sake of preferment, or some imaginary honour, have freely lent a helping hand, to oppress, nay to destroy, their country. . . . This is what every man (who values freedom) ought to consider; he should act by judgment, and not by affection of self-interest; for, where these prevail, no ties of either country or kindred are regarded; as, on the other hand, the man, who loves his country, prefers its liberty to all other considerations; well knowing that, without liberty, life is a misery. . . .

Power may justly be compared to a great river, which, kept within due bounds, is both beautiful and useful; but when it overflows its banks, it is then too impetuous to be stemmed; it bears down all before it, and brings destruction and desolation wherever it comes. If then this is the nature of power, let us at least do our duty, and like wise men (who value freedom) use our utmost care to support liberty, the only bulwark against lawless power, which in all ages has sacrificed to its wild lust and boundless ambition, the blood of the best men that ever lived. . . .

I should think it my duty, if required, to go to the utmost part of the land, where my services could be of any use in assisting to quench the flame of prosecutions upon informations [*accusations*], set on foot by the government, to deprive a people of the right of remonstrating, and complaining of, the arbitrary attempts of men in power. . . . But to conclude; the question before the court and you, gentlemen of the jury, is not of small or private concern, it is not the cause of a poor printer, nor a New-York slave, which you are now trying: No! it may, in its consequences, affect every freeman that lives under a British government on the main of America. It is the best cause; it is the cause of liberty! and I make no doubt but your upright conduct, this day, will not only entitle you to the love and esteem of your fellow-citizens; but every man who prefers freedom to a life of slavery, will bless and honour you, as men who have baffled the attempt of tyranny, and who, by an impartial and incorrupt verdict, have laid a noble foundation for securing to ourselves, our posterity, and our neighbours, That, to which nature and the laws of our country have given us a right,—the liberty—both of exposing and opposing arbitrary power (in these parts of the world at least) by speaking and writing truth.

# WILLIAM LIVINGSTON ON FREEDOM—
AND RESPONSIBILITY—OF THE PRESS
(1753)*

*There were many outstanding spokesmen for the freedom of the press in colonial America—Andrew Hamilton, Colden, Provost William Smith, Franklin, and many others. One of the most powerful was William Livingston, lawyer, politician, educator, and litterateur of New York. In a series of essays in* The Independent Reflector, *Livingston expounded his liberal ideas on many subjects, among them the problem of the freedom of the press. But Livingston recognized the principle that with freedom goes responsibility, that if the press was to enjoy freedom it must discipline itself and not allow its freedom to degenerate into license.*

⚹ ⚹ ⚹

Whether the Art of Printing has been of greater Service or Detriment to the World, has frequently been made the Subject of fruitless Controversy. The best Things have been perverted to serve the vilest Purposes, their being therefore subject to Abuse, is an illogical Argument against their Utility. Before the Invention of the Press, the Progress of Knowledge was slow, because the Methods of diffusing it were laborious and expensive. . . . It is otherwise since the Discovery of the Art of *Printing.* The most inferior Genius, however impoverished, can spread his Thoughts thro' a Kingdom. The Public has the Advantage of the Sentiments of all its Individuals. Thro' the Press, Writers of every Character and Genius, may promulge their Opinions; and all conspire to rear and support the Republic of Letters. The Patriot can by this Means, diffuse his salutary Principles thro' the Breasts of his Countrymen, interpose his friendly Advice unasked, warn them against approaching Danger, write them against the Arm of despotic Power,

* William Livingston, "Of the Use, Abuse, and Liberty of the Press," *The Independent Reflector,* No. XL, Aug. 30, 1753.

and perhaps, at the Expence of but a few Sheets of Paper, save the State from impending Destruction. . . .

It must indeed be confessed, that this useful Discovery has, like many others, been prostituted to serve the basest Ends. . . . But to shut up the Press because it has been abused, would be like burning our Bibles and proscribing our Religion, because its Doctrines have been desobeyed and misrepresented; or like throwing off all Law and Restraint, and sinking into a State of Nature, because the overgrown Power of the Civil Ruler, abusing his Trust, has sacrificed the Lives and Properties of his Subjects, to lawless and tyrannical Sway. . . .

The wide influence of the Press is so dangerous to arbitrary Governments, that in some of them it is shut up, and in others greatly restrained. The Liberty of complaining, of carrying that Complaint to the Throne itself, and of breathing the Sighs of an afflicted, oppressed Nation, has too great a Tendency to produce a Revolution to be suffered in despotic Governments. . . . Power supported without Right, cannot bear, and therefore will not submit itself to a public Examination. Knowledge inspires a love of Liberty,—and Liberty in the People, is incompatable with the Security of an arbitrary Legislator. . . .

No Nation in *Europe,* is more jealous of the *Liberty of the Press* than the *English,* nor is there a People, among whom it is so greatly abused. . . . We are so besotted with the Love of Liberty, that running into Extreams, we even tolerate those Things which naturally tend to its Subversion. . . . The *Liberty of the Press,* like Civil Liberty, is talked of by many, and understood but by few; the latter is taken by multitudes, for an irrefreinable Licence of acting at Pleasure; an equal Unrestraint in Writing, is often argued from the former, but both are false and *equally* dangerous to our Constitution. Civil Liberty is built upon a Surrender of so much of our natural Liberty, as is necessary for the good Ends of Government; and the Liberty of the Press, is always to be restricted from becoming a Prejudice to the public Weal. . . .

This is the true Liberty of the Press for which Englishmen [*in America*] ought to contend. Such a Liberty can never be dangerous, either to the Public, or their Ruler; but on the contrary may often be necessary. . . .

A Printer ought not to publish ever[y] Thing that is offered him, but what is conducive of general Utility, he should not refuse, be the Author a Christian, Jew, Turk or Infidel. Such Refusal is an immediate Abridgement of the Freedom of the Press. When on the other Hand, he prostitutes his Art by the Publication of any Thing injurious to his Country, it is Criminal, —It is high Treason against the State.

# JOHN RANDOLPH ON FREEDOM OF SPEECH IN POLITICAL DEBATE (1734, 1736)*

*John Randolph, for many years speaker of the Virginia House of Burgesses, was a sincere and eloquent defender of the freedom of debate in the Virginia House of Burgesses. He explained why freedom of speech in the legislature was essential to the success of representative government; but his statement of the principle as applied to political matters was echoed in many other areas by other American leaders. The first selection here is from his acceptance speech at the time of his election to the Speakership of the Virginia House of Burgesses in 1734; the second is from his speech to the Governor, as Speaker of the House, in 1736.*

◢        ◢        ◢

(a) But I have abundant Reason to hope, from my experience of the Candor and Good-will of this House towards me, that I shall be exempted from any unkind censures . . . and indeed, seeing we have the Happiness, which seems almost peculiar to our selves, a being under none of the Perturbations which we see every where else arising from the different Views and Designs of Factions and Parties, and have yet no Footsteps of Corruption among us, instead of raising any Heat or Intemperance in our Debates, which are always unnecessary, we should look upon all Differences among us to proceed from the Doubtfulness of Expedients that shall be proposed for the Common Good: And upon that Account the Minority should submit calmly and chearfully to what the Majority determines. . . .

* John Randolph, (a) Acceptance Speech on his election to the Speakership of the Virginia House of Burgesses, August 24, 1734, *Journals of the House of Burgesses of Virginia*, ed. H. R. McIlwaine (Richmond, 1910), p. 176; (b) Speech to the Governor, August 8, 1736, *Ibid., 1736-1740*, pp. 241-242.

Then we shall hear one another patiently, put the Weight of every Man's Reason in the Ballance against our own, and at last form a Judgment upon the whole matter; which, if not the wisest, yet, resulting from the Integrity of our own Principles, will be honest and commendable. . . . And, however Mankind may be provoked, by being thwarted with the Sentiments of other Men, a Variety of Opinions is not only necessary to our Natures, but is likewise of all Things the most useful; since if all Men were of one Mind, there would be no Need of Councils; no Subject of Learning and Eloquence; the Mind would want its proper Exercise, and without it, like the Body, would lose its natural Strength, from a habit of Slothard Idleness. Truth itself will receive an Addition of Strength by being opposed, and can never be in Danger of suffering by the Test of Argument.

(b) The Planters, who sustain'd the Heat and Burthen of the first Settlement of this Plantation, were miserably harassed by the Government, in the Form it was then established [*under the Charter of 1609*], which had an unnatural Power of Ruling by Martial Law, and Constitutions passed by a Council in *England,* without the Consent of the People. . . . And such have been in all Ages, and for ever must continue to be, the Effects of an Arbitrary Despotic Power; of which the Company in *London,* in whom all Dominion and Property was then lodged, were so sensible, that they resolved to establish another form of Government more agreeable and suitable to the Temper and Genius of the *English* Nation. And accordingly, in July, 1621, pass'd a Charter under their Common Seal, . . . whereby they ordered and declared, That . . . there should be Two Supreme Councils; One to be called, *The Council of State,* . . . the other to be called . . . *The General Assembly.* . . .

## — Reading No. 34 —

## A PENNSYLVANIAN'S VIEWS ON THE INTERNATIONAL SITUATION (1732)*

*James Logan of Philadelphia, the Proprietor's personal representative in Pennsylvania, in 1732 wrote a survey of the international situation and the place of the colonies in it. His memorial was sent to London and submitted to Sir Robert Walpole, who was directing British policy. So far as is known, it did not have the influence Logan hoped it might have.*

It is well known that the Power of which Britain has the most reason to be apprehensive, is France, that the Principal Security of Britain consists in its Naval Force, and that this is Supported by its Trade and Navigation. [*It is no*] less certain that these are very much advanced by means of the British Dominions in America: the Preservation of which is therefore of the utmost importance to the Kingdom it Self, for it is manifest that if France could possess itself of those Dominions and thereby become Masters of all their Trade, their Sugars, Tobacco, Rice, Timber and Naval Stores, they would soon be an Overmatch in Naval Strength to the rest of Europe, and then be in a Condition to prescribe Laws to the whole. . . .

This being the present State of the Northern Continent of America towards the Atlantick in respect to their strength and Security, the writer will not Presume to hint at the Remedies proper to be Applied on the part of Britain further than to Observe they will naturally Occur from the Defects that have been Noted. It has indeed been thought by some a Natural

* James Logan, "Of the State of the British Plantations in America. A Memorial." Printed in Joseph C. Johnson, ed., "A Quaker Imperialist's View of the British Colonies in America, 1732," *Pennsylvania Magazine of History and Biography*, Vol. LX, No. 2 (April, 1936), pp. 97-130. Reproduced by permission of the *Pennsylvania Magazine of History and Biography*.

Policy to keep the several Colonies under distinct and independent Commands, the more effectually to Secure them from a Revolt from the Crown. . . . But those who Apprehend any probability of this for Several Ages to come, or while the Mother Countrys in Europe Maintain their Power at Home, indulge their Political Speculations without any just foundation. . . . 'Tis the present Interest of France to make themselves Strong at Home, and its plain that nothing but a Conjunction with Spain could more effectually Contribute to that than the Accession of the Trade & Navigation of America and its very certain that ever since the Peace of Utretcht they have constantly Studied and been Silently making Advances to this while the British Interest there appears to have been as much neglected.

For if leaving the Continent we take a View of the Islands the Subject will appear almost too melancholly to Treat of and the Condition those belonging to British are [in] is so obvious, that it appears impossible it should not be known. The English in the beginning of King William's War invaded Martinico, and soon after that of Queen Anne began they did the same by Guadeloupe, and both to no other purpose than to provoke by their Devastations. But now the French in all those parts are become Vastly more powerful. By their encroachments on and possession of the better parts of Hispaniola and their greater number of Islands, they have much more Ground in the West Indies than Britain, They are much better Fortifyed, more populous more frugal industrious and regular, and which is no Trifle in their Case, much more mildly Treat their Slaves. . . . Thus the French Islands appear now in a Condition in case of a Rupture, to Spare Men Enough of their own without any other Assistance, than Perhaps some Shipping, to make themselves Masters of any one and, in Course, of all the Carribees, nor could Jamaica (humanely Speaking) withstand the Force they could bring against it. But if Spain should join with France in such Attacks it would be impossible otherwise than by large Fleets from Britain to defend them. Could the Court of Spain be brought to consider their true interest it would probably be theirs to keep the Power of France and Britain in the West Indies on a Ballance the better to preserve their own Possessions, but this is at present only speculation.

To conclude, tho' the American Plantations are of such Importance to Britain, that the Loss of them to any other Power especially to France might be its own ruin, . . . on further Proper Inquiries it will appear in what Condition they are at present to defend themselves and how growing the

Danger is of their being Lost without different Measures. In case of a War the Allies of Britain may think themselves less [*obliged?*] to yield [*her*] any Assistance there, and yet there it is manifestly the Interest of France to begin it.

## AN ENGLISH COLONIAL GOVERNOR CORRESPONDS WITH A FRENCH COLONIAL GOVERNOR ABOUT INTERNATIONAL ISSUES (1749)*

*William Shirley, governor of Massachusetts, undertook a vigorous correspondence, in 1749, with the Marquis de la Galissonière, governor of French Canada, with regard to the situation in Nova Scotia, where the Indians under French tutelage had committed a number of ravages upon the English there. Similar exchanges between English colonial governors and French or Spanish governors were frequent throughout the colonial period. They usually had to do either with Indian affairs or with rival territorial claims. Both Shirley and Galissonière were presently named by their respective governments as members of the Anglo-French joint commission set up under the Treaty of Aix-la-Chapelle to settle a boundary between the two empires in North America.*

ᐩ     ᐩ     ᐩ

For this perfidious behaviour [*of the Indians of Nova Scotia*] I caus'd war to be declared in His Majesty's name against these Indians, at Boston, in November 1744, and, so far as it depends on me, they shall not be admitted, Sir, to terms of peace, till they have made a proper submission for their treachery, unless they should be already comprehended in the Definitive Treaty of Peace and Friendship lately concluded at Aix la Chapelle; which I shall on my part strictly observe on every point.

As to what you have thought fit, Sir, to declare in your letter concerning your intentions to support the Indians in acts of hostility against us, unless we give 'em peace upon the terms

* William Shirley to the Marquis de la Galissonière, May 9, 1749. E. B. O'Callaghan, ed., *Documents Relative to the Colonial History of the State of New York* (15 vols., Albany, 1856-1887), Vol. VI, pp. 483-484.

there prescribed by you, and the danger the frontiers of the Massachusetts Bay in particular may be in, unless you have a speedy and positive answer upon this head; what I have to say in answer is, That I shall be sorry for a new rupture between us, and am very desirous to have perfect tranquillity restored to the Province under my government; but if the latter is not to be the case and you think fit to make yourself a party in an Indian war against us; I doubt not but His Majesty's subjects upon this Continent will be able to make just reprizalls upon Canada, when it shall be His Majesty's pleasure to have 'em do it. . . .

The right you claim, Sir, of sending Missionaries from France to reside among His Majesty's subjects of Nova Scotia as their priests, and in consequence of that, your forbidding His Majesty's Governor [*Mascarene*] to make any alteration in the State of Religion and it's Ministers there, is still more extraordinary, and I must not omit upon this occasion to remark to you that I think the letter which the Bishop of Quebec lately wrote to Mr. Mascarene concerning his intended invitation of His Majesty's subjects in that government in such terms as shewed he looks upon 'em as a part of his cure of souls and within his jurisdiction, was likewise an extraordinary attempt and can't be admitted. . . .

I can't conclude without making use of this opportunity to acquaint you, Sir, that we [*also*] look upon Fort St. Frederick at Crown Point [*on Lake Champlain*] as an encroachment upon His Majesty's territories, and in case you proceed to settle the country round it, shall esteem those settlements so too, unless that tract has been ceded to you by the late Definitive Treaty at Aix la Chapelle.

# THE REV. JONATHAN MAYHEW DEMANDS THE ELIMINATION OF THE FRENCH FROM NORTH AMERICA (1754)*

*The intensity of the feeling of many Angloamericans that the conflict with the French in North America was insoluble, and that, therefore, the French must be driven out of the continent, reached what was perhaps its most extreme expression in the election sermon of Rev. Jonathan Mayhew in 1754. Mayhew was convinced that coexistence with the French was impossible, on three grounds: First, the French political system was absolutist: under it there could be no freedom; if it should prevail over the English in North America, they would lose their liberties and become political slaves. Second, the French were Roman Catholics; this meant, to the New England Congregationalist, "priest-craft" and persecution; Catholicism was anathema, a religious system that was devoted to the devices of Satan. Third, the occupation of the continent by the French, even the interior parts of it, would mean blocking the natural and God-willed expansion of the British society, characterized by "British liberties," westward. The rationalization of Angloamerican imperialism was thus based upon religious, politico-cultural, and territorial considerations.*

✶     ✶     ✶

That which seems, at present, chiefly to engage the attention of the public, is the British settlements on the Continent being now, in a manner, encompassed by the French. And this is a matter of much more serious importance than it would be, were it not for the numerous tribes of warlike natives on our back; who, it is to be feared, are more generally disposed to fall in with that interest, than with ours. . . .

---

* Jonathan Mayhew, *A Sermon Preach'd in the Audience of His Excellency William Shirley, Esq; . . . ,* May 29th, 1754 (Boston, 1754), pp. 32-47.

The warlike preparations that are made and making, in our southern colonies, prove that they are not unapprehensive of what may be the consequence of those quick advances & gigantic strides, which the French are making towards us; the consequence of the strict alliances they are forming with those Indians who are already our enemies; of their endeavours to secure such as are yet neuters; and of their practices, and many artifices, to corrupt those who are in amity with us. . . .

And, indeed, the progress they have made in a short time, might seem strange, were it not for their union amongst themselves, and for the nature of their government. The slaves are content to starve at home, in order to injure free-men abroad, and to extend their territories by violence and usurpation. Their late conduct may well alarm us; especially considering our disunion, or at least want of a sufficient bond of union, amongst ourselves: An inconvenience, which, it is to be hoped, we shall not always labour under. And whenever all our scattered rays shall be drawn to a point and proper focus, they can scarce fail to consume and burn up these enemies of our peace, how faintly soever they may strike at present. What Union can do, we need only look towards those Provinces, which are distinguished by the name of the United, to know. But in the mean time, each government that considers its own true interest, will undoubtly concur in such measures as are necessary and practicable, for the common safety. . . .

And what horrid scene is this, which restless, roving fancy, or something of an higher nature, presents to me; and so chills my blood! Do I behold these territories of freedom, become the prey of arbitrary power? Do I see the motly armies of French and painted Salvages, taking our fortresses, and erecting their own, even in our capital towns and cities! Do I behold them spreading desolation thro' the land! Do I see the slaves of Lewis with their Indian allies, dispossessing the free-born subjects of King George, of the inheritance received from their forefathers, and purchased by them at the expence of their ease, their treasure, their blood! To aggravate the indignity beyond human toleration, do I see this goodly patrimony ravished from them, by those who never knew what property was, except by seizing that of others for an insatiable Lord! Do I see christianity banished for popery! the bible, for the mass-book! the oracles of truth, for fabulous legends! Do I see the sacred Edifices erected here to the honour of the true God, and his Son, on the ruins of pagan superstition and idolatry; erected here, *where Satan's seat was;* do I see these sacred Edifices laid in ruins themselves! and others rising in their places, consecrated to the honour of saints and angels! Instead of a train of Christ's faithful, laborious ministers, do I behold

an herd of lazy Monks, and Jesuits, and Exorcists, and Inquisi-
tors, and cowled, and uncowled Impostors! Do I see a protestant, there, stealing a look at his bible, and being taken in the
fact, punished like a felon! What indignity is yonder offered to
the matrons! and here, to the virgins! Is it now a crime to
reverence the hoary head! And is he alone happy, that taketh
the little ones, and dasheth them against the stones! Do I see
all liberty, property, religion, happiness, changed, or rather
transubstantiated, into slavery, poverty, superstition, wretched-
ness! And, in fine, do I hear the miserable sufferers (those of
them that survive) bitterly accusing the negligence of the public
Guardians! and charging all their calamities, less upon the enemies, than upon the fathers, of their country! O dishonest!
profane! execrable sight! O piercing sound! that *entereth into
the ears of the Lord of* Sabbaoth! Where! in what region! in
what world am I! Is this imagination? (its own busy tormentor)
Or is it something more divine? I will not, I cannot believe
'tis prophetic vision; or that God has so far abandoned us! . . .

. . . Peace is a great blessing; peace is what we would chuse;
peace is the desire of all who deserve the name of Christians.
But shall the trumpet sleep? Shall the sword rust? Shall our
gold and silver lye cankering in our coffers? Shall our military
garments be moth-eaten for want of use, when such things are
doing! It is impossible, Gentlemen, you should be any ways
backward, or parsimonious, in such a cause as this; a cause
wherein the glory of God, the honour of your King, and the
good of your country, are so deeply concerned; I might perhaps
add, a cause, whereon the liberties of Europe depend. For of
so great consequence is the empire of North America, (and that,
you are sensible, is the thing now aimed at by our neighbours)
that it must turn the scale of power greatly in favour of the
only Monarch, from whom those liberties are in danger; and
against that Prince, who is the grand support and bulwark of
them. Consider then, Gentlemen, in the name of God, consider, what you owe Him, and to your holy religion; what, to
the protestant interest in general; what, to your King and to
Great-Britain, in particular; what, to your native country; what,
to the honour of your Ancestors; what, to the present generation; what, to future ones; what, to yourselves; and what, to
those whom the God of nature has made dearer to you than
yourselves, your children. It is even uncertain, Gentlemen, how
long you will have an House to sit in, unless a speedy and
vigorous opposition is made to the present encroachments, and
to the farther designs, of our enemies! This, surely, is not a
time to be saving, unless in our private expences.

## — Reading No. 37 —

## COTTON MATHER SEES ANGLOAMERICA AS THE CULMINATION OF THE DIVINE PLAN (1709)*

*Cotton Mather was convinced that New England, at least, was founded in response to a direct intention of God. In his sermon* Theopolis Americana (American City of God) *he explained the divine intention. His was a religious form of American self-consciousness that was shared by Jonathan Edwards and others in New England. American self-consciousness in other colonies, and later, was generally of a more secular sort.*

    ✓              ✓              ✓

Glorious Things are Spoken of Thee, O thou City of God [*illegible*] Street be in [*Thee*] O New England; The Interpretation of it, be unto you, O American Colonies. . . .
There are many Arguments to perswade us That our Glorious Lord, will have an Holy City in America; a City, the Street whereof shall be Pure Gold. . . . There have been Martyrs of Christ in America. The Blood of the Martyrs here, is an Omen that the Truths for which they Suffered are to Rise, and Live, and carry all before them, in the Land that hath been so marked for the Lord. . . . But our Glorious Lord, will order that Good Seed ere long, to be cast, upon the Fertile Regions of America, and it shall here find a Good Ground, where it shall bring forth Fruit unto astonishments; and unto Perpetuity. . . .

* Cotton Mather, *Theopolis Americana* (Boston, 1710), pp. 1, 41, 45-46.

# REV. SAMUEL DAVIES ON RELIGION AND PATRIOTISM (1755)*

*The outbreak of war with the French in North America in 1754 and 1755 terrified the people along the western frontiers of Angloamerica, from Nova Scotia to Georgia. Everywhere, there were calls to arms and to preparedness. In western Virginia the Reverend Samuel Davies, Presbyterian minister in Hanover County and later president of Princeton College, exhorted the militia to rise and fight valiantly against the French and Indians in the name of "patriotism" for their "country" (Virginia). Like Jonathan Mayhew in Massachusetts, Davies justified religious endorsement of warfare against these enemies on grounds of "liberty," of religion, and of the cause of civilization against savagery.*

✦     ✦     ✦

[*The French and their savage allies are ravaging our borders;*] and shall these Savages go unchecked? Shall Virginia incur the Guilt and the everlasting shame, of tamely exchanging her Liberty, her Religion, and her All, for arbitrary Gallic Power, and for Popish Slavery, Tyranny and Massacre? Alas! are there none of her children, that enjoyed all the blessings of her Peace, that will espouse her Cause, and befriend her now, in the Time of her Danger? Are Britons utterly degenerated by so short a Remove from their Mother-Country? Is the Spirit of Patriotism entirely extinguished among us? And must I give thee up for lost, O my Country, and all that is included in that important Word? Must I look upon thee as a conquered, enslaved Province of France and the Range of Indian Savages? My Heart breaks at the Thought and must ye, our unhappy Brethren in our Frontiers, must ye stand the single Barrier of a ravaged Country, unassisted, unbefriended, unpitied? Alas! must I draw these shocking Conclusions? . . .

* Samuel Davies, *Religion and Patriotism the Constituents of a Good Soldier* (Philadelphia, 1755), pp. 5-14.

While I have you before me, I have high Thoughts of a Virginian; and I entertain the pleasing Hope that my Country may yet emerge out of her Distress, and flourish with her usual Blessings. . . .

Our Continent is like to become the Seat of War; and we, for the future (till the sundry European Nations that have planted Colonies in it, have fixed their Boundaries by the Sword) have no other Way left to defend our Rights and Privileges. And has God been pleased to diffuse some Sparks of this Martial Fire through our Country? I hope he has. . . .

To protect your Brethren from the most bloody Barbarities— to defend the Territories of the best of Kings against the Oppression and Tyranny of arbitrary Power to secure the inestimable Blessings of Liberty, British Liberty, from the chains of French Slavery—to preserve your Estates, for which you have sweat and toiled, from falling a Prey to greedy Vultures, Indians, Priests, French, and hungry Gallic Slaves, or not-more-devouring Flames—to guard your Religion, the pure Religion of Jesus, streaming uncorrupted from the sacred Fountain of the Scriptures; the most excellent, rational and divine Religion that ever was made known to the Sons of Men; to guard such a precious Religion (my Heart grows warm while I mention it) against Ignorance, Superstition, Idolatry, Tyranny over Conscience, Massacre, Fire and Sword, and all the Mischiefs, beyond Expression, with which Popery is Pregnant—to keep from the cruel Hands of Barbarians and Papists your Wives, your Children, your Parents, your Friends—to secure the Liberties conveyed to you by your brave Fore-Fathers, and bought with their Blood, that you may transmit them uncurtailed to your Posterity—these are the Blessings you contend for; all these will be torn from your eager Grasp, if this Colony should become a Province of France. And Virginians! Britons! Christians! Protestants! if these Names have any Import or Energy, will you not strike home in such a Cause? . . .

# NATHANIAL AMES SALUTES THE FUTURE AMERICA (1758)*

*Nathanial Ames of Boston, one of the great American almanac publishers of the eighteenth century, had a strong sense of the "manifest destiny" of Angloamerica to grow into a great culture. In his almanac,* Astronomical Diary, *for the year 1758, he published the following salute to the "unborn Inhabitants of America" of "two or three Centuries" later— that is, 1958 or 2058!*

The Curious have observ'd, that the Progress of Humane Literature (like the Sun) is from the East to the West; thus has it travelled thro' Asia and Europe, and now is arrived at the Eastern Shore of America. As the Coelestial Light of the Gospel was directed here by the Finger of GOD, it will doubtless, finally drive the long! long! Night of Heathenish Darkness from America:—So Arts and Sciences will change the Face of Nature in their Tour from Hence over the Appalachian Mountains to the Western Ocean; and as they march thro' the vast Desert, the Residence of wild Beasts will be broken up, and their obscene Howl cease for ever;—Instead of which, the Stones and Trees will dance together at the Music of Orpheus. —The Rocks will disclose their hidden Gems,—and the inestimable Treasures of Gold & Silver be broken up. Huge Mountains of Iron Ore are already discovered; and vast Stores are reserved for future Generations: This Metal more useful than Gold and Silver, will employ millions of Hands, not only to form the martial Sword, and peaceful Share, alternately; but an Infinity of Utensils improved in the Exercise of Art, and Handicraft amongst Men. Nature thro' all her Works has stamp'd Authority on this Law, namely, "That all fit Matter shall be improved to its best Purposes."—Shall not then those

* Nathanial Ames, *An Astronomical Diary for the Year 1758* (Boston, 1757).

vast Quarries, that team with mechanic Stone,—those for Structure be piled into great Cities,—and those for Sculpture into Statues to perpetuate the Honor of renowned Heroes; even those who shall now save their Country,—*O! Ye unborn Inhabitants of America! Should this Page escape its destin'd Conflagration at the Year's End, and these Alphabetical Letters remain legible,—when your Eyes behold the Sun after he has rolled the Seasons round for two or three Centuries more, you will know that in* Anno Domini 1758, *we dream'd of your Times.*

# THE RISING GLORY OF AMERICA (1771)*

*The growing sense of the cultural uniqueness and destiny of America found eloquent poetic expression in the Princeton commencement poem, composed by Philip Freneau and Hugh H. Brackenridge. It is a long poem; the essential sense of it is conveyed in the following lines.*

To mighty nations shall the people grow
Which cultivate the banks of many a flood,
In chrystal currents poured from the hills
Apalachia nam'd, to lave the sands
Of Carolina, Georgia, and the plains
Stretch'd out from thence far to the burning Line,
St. Johns or Clarendon or Albemarle. . . .

And here fair freedom shall forever reign.
I see a train, a glorious train appear,
Of Patriots plac'd in equal fame with those
Who nobly fell for Athens or for Rome.

This is thy praise America thy pow'r
Thou best of climes by science visited
By freedom blest and richly stor'd with all
The luxuries of life. Hail happy land
The seat of empire the abode of kings,
The final stage where time shall introduce
Renowned characters, and glorious works
Of high invention and of wond'rous art,
While not the ravages of time shall waste
Till he himself has run his long career;
Till all those glorious orbs of light on high
The rolling wonders that surround the ball,
Drop from their spheres extinguish'd and consum'd,
When final ruin with her fiery car
Rides o'er creation, and all natures works
Are lost in chaos and the womb of night.

* Philip Freneau and Hugh Henry Brackenridge, *Poem on the Rising Glory of America* (Philadelphia, 1772), pp. 22-23.

# SELECTED BIBLIOGRAPHY

BERNARD BAILYN, *Education in the Forming of American Society* (Chapel Hill, 1960).

CARL BRIDENBAUGH, editor, *Gentleman's Progress: The Itinerarium of Dr. Alexander Hamilton, 1744* (Chapel Hill, 1948).

I. BERNARD COHEN, *Franklin and Newton* (Philadelphia, 1956).

MICHEL-GUILLAUME ST. JEAN DE CRÈVECOEUR, *Letters From an American Farmer* (London, 1926).

JOSEPH DORFMAN, *The Economic Mind in American Civilization, 1606-1918,* Vol. I (New York, 1949).

ERNEST EARNEST, *John and William Bartram* (Philadelphia, 1940).

BENJAMIN FRANKLIN, *The Papers of Benjamin Franklin,* edited by Leonard W. Labaree (5 vols. to date. New Haven, 1959-    ).

EDWIN S. GAUSTAD, *The Great Awakening in New England* (New York, 1957).

MARCUS LEE HANSEN, *The Atlantic Migration, 1607-1860* (Cambridge, 1940).

BROOKE HINDLE, *The Pursuit of Science in Revolutionary America, 1735-1789* (Chapel Hill, 1956).

THEODORE HORNBERGER, *Scientific Thought in the American Colleges, 1638-1800* (Austin, 1945).

HANS KOHN, *American Nationalism* (New York, 1957).

LEONARD W. LABAREE, *Conservatism in Early American History* (New York, 1948).

LEONARD W. LABAREE, *Royal Government in America* (New Haven, 1930).

PERRY MILLER, *Jonathan Edwards* (New York, 1949).

PERRY MILLER, *The New England Mind: From Colony to Province* (Cambridge, 1953).

PERRY MILLER, *The New England Mind: The Seventeenth Century* (Cambridge, 1954).

HERBERT MORAIS, *Deism in Eighteenth Century America* (New York, 1934).

SAMUEL E. MORISON, *The Intellectual Life of Colonial New England* (New York, 1956).

V. L. PARRINGTON, *The Colonial Mind, 1620-1800* (*Main Currents in American Thought*. 3 vols. New York, 1927-1930, Vol. I).

I. W. RILEY, *American Philosophy: The Early Schools* (New York, 1907).

CLINTON ROSSITER, *Conservatism in America* (New York, 1955).

CLINTON ROSSITER, *Seedtime of the Republic* (New York, 1953).

MAX SAVELLE, "The American Balance of Power and European Diplomacy, 1713-1778," in R. B. Morris, editor, *The Era of the American Revolution* (New York, 1939), pp. 140-169.

MAX SAVELLE, "Nationalism and Other Loyalties in the American Revolution," *American Historial Review*, Vol. LXVII, No. 4 (July, 1962), pp. 901-923.

MAX SAVELLE, *Seeds of Liberty* (New York, 1948).

HERBERT SCHNEIDER, *A History of American Philosophy* (New York, 1946).

ABBOT EMERSON SMITH, *Colonists in Bondage* (Chapel Hill, 1947).

R. E. SPILLER, *et al., Literary History of the United States,* Vol. I (New York, 1953).

GERALD B. STOURZH, *Benjamin Franklin and American Diplomacy* (Chicago, 1954).

DIRK J. STRUIK, *Yankee Science in the Making* (Boston, 1948).

W. W. SWEET, *Religion in Colonial America* (New York, 1942).

MOSES C. TYLER, *A History of American Literature, 1607-1765* (2 vols. in one. New York, 1881).

JOHN WOOLMAN, *The Journal of John Woolman,* edited by Janet Whitney (Chicago, 1950).

CONRAD WRIGHT, *The Beginnings of Unitarianism in America* (Boston, 1955).

LOUIS B. WRIGHT, *The Cultural Life of the American Colonies, 1607-1763* (New York, 1957).

LOUIS B. WRIGHT, *The First Gentlemen of Virginia* (San Marino, 1940).

# INDEX